Ethical eye

Euthanasia

Volume I – Ethical and human aspects

French version:

Regard éthique – L'Euthanasie
Volume I – Aspects éthiques et humains

ISBN: 92-871-5069-9

Cover design: Graphic Design Workshop, Council of Europe
Photo: Christophe Hamm
Layout: Desktop Publishing Unit, Council of Europe

Edited by Council of Europe Publishing
http://book.coe.int

Council of Europe Publishing
F-67075 Strasbourg Cedex

ISBN 92-871-5070-2
© Council of Europe, September 2003
Printed in Germany

Contents

Contributors

Philippe Letellier

Philippe Letellier is a lecturer at the Faculty of Medicine in Caen and Head of the Internal Medicine Department, where he runs a small palliative care ward. He also runs a university course for doctors and nurses, leading to a university qualification in palliative care. The course comprises several seminars in which all aspects of palliative care are studied: ethical, philosophical, anthropological and, of course, the medical and technical aspects. Philippe Letellier is also a member of the National College of Palliative Care Teachers.

Jean-Paul Harpes

Jean-Paul Harpes was formerly a Professor of Philosophy at Luxemburg University. He is currently President of the Luxemburg Commission Nationale d'Ethique (CNE), of which he was the co-ordinator for eight years. He is also president of a national consultative committee (CRRC) on conflict prevention and resolution. His research focuses on problems concerning ethics, democracy and human rights and he is the author of numerous publications in these fields.

Göran Hermerén

Professor of Medical Ethics at the Faculty of Medicine, Lund University, Sweden, since 1991 and Professor of Philosophy at Lund University since 1975, Göran Hermerén is co-ordinator of the EU-funded research project Euro-priorities. He has published several books and papers on ethical problems in international periodicals. Current research interests include ethical aspects of gene testing and stem cell research. He is member of the National Council of Medical Ethics in Sweden, Chairman of the Ethics Committee of the Swedish Research Council (Stockholm), Chairman of the Advisory Board of the German Reference Centre for Ethics in the Life Sciences DRZE (Bonn) and President of the European Group on Ethics in Science and New Technologies (Brussels).

Nicolas Aumonier

Nicolas Aumonier lectures in history and the philosophy of sciences at Joseph Fourier University (Grenoble I, France). Formerly a student at the Ecole Normale Supérieure, *agrégé* in philosophy, a former member of Antoine Danchin's Regulation of Gene Expression Laboratory (Institut Pasteur, Paris) and Doctor of Philosophy at the Paris-I-Panthéon-Sorbonne University, he is currently working on the history and philosophy of contemporary biology. Since 1991, he has been a member of the Advisory Committee on the Protection of Individuals in Biomedical Research (Paris-Hôpital Saint-Antoine) and has published several works on the ethics of biomedical research and on euthanasia.

Tony O'Brien

Dr Tony O'Brien is Medical Director of Marymount Hospice, Cork, and Consultant Physician in Palliative Medicine at Cork University Hospital. Trained at St Christopher's Hospice, London, Dr O'Brien returned to Ireland in 1991 to take up his current post. He is Chairman of the Council of Europe Committee of Experts on the Organisation of Palliative Care, and also chaired the National Advisory Committee on Palliative Care in Ireland. He is particularly interested in the development of palliative care services, ethical issues and in the provision of specialist palliative care services to patients with non-malignant diseases.

Georg Marckmann

Georg Marckmann studied medicine and philosophy at the University of Tübingen, Germany, and was also a scholar at the "Ethics in the Sciences and Humanities" Postgraduate College in Tübingen. Since 1998 he has been Assistant Professor at the Institute of Ethics and History of Medicine at the University of Tübingen. From 1999 to 2000 he studied public health at Harvard School of Public Health in Boston, MA. His main research interests are philosophical and methodological issues in medical ethics, clinical ethics, distributive justice and priorities in health care, and computer-based decision support in medicine and telemedicine.

Bernard Kouchner

Bernard Kouchner first qualified as a gastroenterologist. In 1971 he founded Médecins sans frontières and then in 1980 "Médecins du monde", an international charity which brings medical relief to the populations most in need, thanks to the commitment of voluntary doctors and other health workers. He himself has taken part in many humanitarian missions. In July 1999, after being Minister of State for Social Integration, Minister of State for Humanitarian Action and finally Minister for Health in 1992, he was appointed Special Representative of the Secretary General and Head of the UN Interim Administration Mission in Kosovo. In January 2001, he left Kosovo and again was appointed Minister for Health in Lionel Jospin's government. He is a professor at CNAM (Paris) and holds the chair in Health and Development.

Christian Byk

Christian Byk is a judge and Vice-President of the Regional Court of Bobigny, France. For fifteen years he was a legal adviser for international affairs at the Ministry of Justice and, in this context, headed delegations to various international bodies, including the Council of Europe and in particular to the Steering Committee on Bioethics. From 1991 until 1993 he was Special Adviser on Bioethics to the Council of Europe Secretary General. Since 1989 he has been responsible for the International Association of Law Ethics and Science, and Vice-President of the Council for International Organisations of Medical Sciences. He is also editor-in-chief of the *International Journal of Bioethics* and the author of numerous works in the field of health and international law.

Daniel Chevassut

Physician at the Centre Hospitalier Régional Universitaire Nord de Marseille, Daniel Chevassut is also founder and organiser of a pain clinic at Hôpital Nord de Marseille. He is a representative of and speaker for the Union Bouddhiste de France on the "Health care ethics, human rights and morality" course at the Université Pierre et Marie Curie-Paris VI.

Gabriella Gambino

Gabriella Gambino has a doctorate in political sciences as well as a doctorate in bioethics from the Bioethics Institute, Université Catholique du Sacré Coeur, in Rome. She is currently carrying out research in bioethics at the Luiss Guido Carli University, Rome. In 2002 she was appointed expert of the scientific secretariat of the National Committee for Bioethics. She also teaches at the Université Catholique du Sacré Coeur.

Raoutsi Hadj Eddine Sari Ali

Raoutsi Hadj Eddine Sari Ali is a member of the European Federation of Scientific Networks (FER) and a lecturer in the school of medicine in Paris. He also broadcasts weekly on Radio France Maghreb on religious education in a secular environment *("L'esprit des religions")*.

Albert Guigui

Albert Guigui is the Chief Rabbi of Brussels and of the Central Israeli Consistory of Brussels. He is co-author of numerous articles and books and has contributed a chapter on Judaism and bioethics in an encyclopaedia on bioethics.

Alexandre M. Stavropoulos

A Professor of Theology and Psychology at the Faculty of Theology, University of Athens, Alexandre Stavropoulos is currently in charge of the postgraduate research programme: "Pastoral theology and education". He is an active member of numerous associations and scientific committees in Greece and elsewhere.

Jean-François Collange

Jean-François Collange is Professor of Ethics at the Faculty of Protestant Theology, Marc Bloch University, Strasbourg, and, since 1996, a member of the Ethics Committee of the French Protestant Federation and of the French National Consultative

Committee on Ethics. Dean of the Faculty of Protestant Theology from 1996 to 2000, he is also the author of several books and numerous papers on the relationship between theology and human rights. Since autumn 2003 he has been chair of the board of the Lutheran Church for Alsace and Lorraine.

Preface

by Walter Schwimmer
Secretary General of the Council of Europe

The fourth book in the "Ethical eye" series focuses on euthanasia, a subject that has been widely discussed across Europe. We all have to face the prospect of death, and how that should be managed arouses our deepest personal feelings as well as engaging the most profound moral and theological beliefs. It is not surprising therefore that the question of euthanasia is passionately debated, and that different individuals, and different states, have reached different conclusions on this issue.

This book does not aim to provide a definitive answer to the question of euthanasia. Rather, it aims to contribute to the political and public debates on this issue by drawing together reflections on the range of ethical and human dimensions that are relevant to the question (Volume I) and reviewing the position both at the European level and in a number of different countries (Volume II). These reviews illustrate the different legal approaches to issues relevant to euthanasia that are in place at present, including refusal of or withdrawing treatment, assisted suicide, and active interventions to end life. The review of the work of the Parliamentary Assembly shows that these issues remain under active consideration by parliamentarians as well as by the wider public.

As was shown in the Council of Europe's survey of the law and practice of member states in this field, which is also reviewed in volume II, there is no single agreed definition of "euthanasia". Therefore, this book takes a wide perspective on medical decision-making at the end of life. In that context, it is clear that there is already a consensus on the value and importance of palliative care at the end of life, even whilst other aspects of end of life decision-making remain actively under debate.

The importance of these issues is acknowledged by all, and it is my hope that this book will contribute to the continuing reflections on this issue at both the national and the European level.

History and definition of a word[1]

by Philippe Letellier

Down the centuries people's attitude to death changed very little : Roland, Don Quixote and Tolstoy's *mujiks* all sensed its approach and took to their sickbeds to await the end. Death was "both familiar and near, evoking no great fear or awe, [and] public [...] with no great show of emotion". But chiefly since the mid-nineteenth century, and "despite the apparent continuity of themes and ritual, death has been furtively pushed out of the world of familiar things" (Ariès, 1959).

It has now become so frightful that we dare not utter its name. It is taboo, a hidden phenomenon. Death has gone under cover, in old people's homes, hospices and hospitals – the places where almost 80% of people die nowadays, not all of whose families are short of space at home. At the same time, medical technology lengthens the uncertain interval between life and death – interminably, some would say (Chaunu, 1978). In many cases it has dehumanised that interval, denying the terminally ill their deaths despite their desire to remain conscious.

Doctors are asked to make death easier, and are increasingly able to do so. Now they are also being asked to cause death in order to cut short suffering. This development is reflected in the history of the word "euthanasia" and the semantic shift it has undergone.

History of the word "euthanasia"

In the history of the word and its use, we find four distinct senses : first, the art of gentle death, and then utilitarian, eugenic and compassionate euthanasia.

From the ancient world to the nineteenth century : the gentle death

Kratinos, a Greek poet writing in the fifth century BC, used the adverb "euthanatôs" to describe a "good death" and particularly a gentle death. The historian Suetonius (AD 63-14) describes how the Emperor Augustus, dying quickly and without suffering in the arms of his wife, Livia, experienced the euthanasia he had wished for.[2]

1.
This article, written in collaboration with Nicolas Aumonier and Bernard Beignier, is based in part on our joint work : Aumonier, Beignier and Letellier, 2001, pp. 7-9 and 35-52.

2.
See Suetonius (AD 70-circa 122), "Augustus", The twelve Caesars, p. 99.

In the Middle Ages, much devotion was associated with caring for and supporting the dying: "Brotherhoods of Good Death" were set up to help the dying and provide support to families in mourning. This tradition is an integral aspect of the Church's function in the Western world.

It was the English statesman and philosopher Francis Bacon (1561-1626) who first used the word "euthanasia" in a medical context to denote death "after the fashion of [...] a kindly and pleasant sleep" (Bacon, 1605). Bacon affirmed that the role of doctors was "not only to restore health, but to mitigate pain and dolours; and not only when such mitigation may conduce to recovery, but when it may serve to make a fair and easy passage". Dying patients were not to be abandoned but were to be given every possible care to help them leave the world more gently and easily (Bacon, 1623). This was the predominant meaning of the word until the nineteenth century. It accurately describes the aim of modern palliative care.

The nineteenth century and utilitarian euthanasia

Jeremy Bentham (1748-1832) and John Stuart Mill (1806-73), representing the doctrine of utilitarianism with its "principle of utility" (Mill, 1863), held that happiness – "pleasure and absence of pain" – was the only thing desirable as an end. When the sum of pain exceeded the sum of pleasure, life became pointless and could be terminated. History contains many examples of suicide or arranged death of people with severe disabilities, of old people once they became burdens on their families, and even (among the Spartans and Romans, for example) of new-born babies with deformities, whom the paterfamilias ordered to be exposed – abandoned – in a desolate place.[1] Such practices have existed among the Eskimos and in Africa and Japan. However, they do not seem to have been present in the Western Judaeo-Christian world until modern times.

The twentieth century : eugenic euthanasia and compassionate euthanasia

Eugenic euthanasia

1.
See Plutarch, *Parallel lives*, I.

The 1830s saw the growth of a health education movement whose aims were to improve the "health and morals" of the

working classes. Following on from this, in 1883, Sir Francis
Galton (1822-1911), a cousin of Charles Darwin, founded the
"science of eugenics" (from the Greek "eu", good, and "genos",
race) with the twin aims of restricting growth in the numbers
of ill-adapted people and improving the race by encouraging
reproduction among the best adapted. In 1895 a book
appeared in Germany with the title *Das Recht auf den Tod* (The
right to death),[1] arguing that certain people's lives had only a
"negative value". In 1913, Charles Richet, winner of the Nobel
Prize in Physiology or Medicine, wrote in *La sélection humaine*
(Richet, 1919) that after elimination of inferior races, the next
step in the selection process was to eliminate people with
abnormalities. In 1920, jurist Karl Ludwig Binding and psychiatrist Alfred Hoche published *Die Freigabe der Vernichtung
lebensunwerten Lebens* (Permission to destroy life that is not
worth living).[2]

Enthusiasm for eugenics spread rapidly in academic circles
and among the public. Between 1900 and 1940, laws were
passed in many countries (Germany, Finland, Sweden and
Norway, as well as thirty-five states of the United States of
America) permitting the sterilisation of people with conditions
that were supposedly hereditary or dangerous to society
(Lecourt, 1996). Hitler took up the same ideas in *Mein Kampf*
in 1924. In 1933, 500 eugenicists from all over the world met
in Bremen to discuss the concept of "life not worth living". In
1935, Alexis Carrel, winner of the Nobel Prize in Medicine and
author of the bestseller *Men, the unknown,* expressed the same
ideas: "None should marry a human being suffering from hidden hereditary defects. [...] Obviously, those who are afflicted
with a heavy ancestral burden of insanity, feeblemindedness
or cancer should not marry. [...] The free practice of eugenics
could lead not only to the development of stronger individuals,
but also of strains [that] should constitute an aristocracy, from
which great men would probably appear" (Carrel, 1935). In
September 1939, Hitler launched a project called "*Aktion* T4",
also known as "Aktion Gnadentod", with the aim of bringing
(literally) "merciful death" to people with mental and physical
disabilities and old people. By the time it was suspended on
24 August 1941 – due to mounting public opposition – Aktion
T4 is believed to have cost the lives of more than 100 000 people
with mental disabilities and some 75 000 old people.[3]

1.
Quoted in Abiven et
al., 2000, p. 37.

2.
Op. cit., p. 37.

3.
See, in particular, Ter-
non, Y., *Le Massacre
des aliénés, des
théoriciens nazis aux
praticiens SS*, Caster-
man, 1971; Abiven et
al., 2000, pp. 36-44;
and Aumonier, Beignier
and Letellier, 2001,
pp. 41-42.

Compassionate euthanasia: some examples and the role of associations

Six Russians who had been bitten by a mad wolf were once sent to Louis Pasteur, who had just finished developing his anti-bacterial serum (1886). The serum failed to work and after days of intolerable agony the men begged Pasteur to end their suffering. Leon Daudet records that, after consulting the pharmacist and the head of the hospital, Pasteur resolved to grant their request. The pharmacist prepared five pills – one of the six men having died already – and these were given to the remaining victims with all the discretion customary in such cases. In the silence that followed the deaths, all present wept with horror. Daudet reports that they were distraught and overwhelmed.[1]

In French literature a similar case of euthanasia is depicted in the death of Thibault père whose doctor son, Antoine, exhausted after days and nights of watching his father's hellish suffering, administers a fatal injection of morphine.[2]

The 1930s saw the emergence of associations advocating compassionate euthanasia: in the UK the Voluntary Euthanasia Association, later known as Exit, was set up in 1935; in the United States, the Society for the Right to Die (SDR) was formed in 1938 and in 1975 renamed itself the Euthanasia Society of America. In the post-war period, and particularly from the 1970s onwards, similar associations sprang up in most parts of the world. Today, under the umbrella of the World Federation of Right-to-Die Societies, they have around 500 000 members in total, 25 000 in France and 60 000 in Switzerland. In 1974 a group of academics, including three Nobel Prize winners, published a manifesto in the French daily *Le Figaro* making the case for a right to euthanasia. In 1979 an article by Michel Lee Lauda, entitled "Un droit" (A right), appeared in *Le Monde*, in which the author argued that very seriously ill patients, people with disabilities and the old had to be given the right to die voluntarily and to be assisted in doing so.

In 1980 the Association for the Right to Die with Dignity (ADMD) was set up in France (branches were created in Spain in 1984 and in Italy in 1986). Article 1 of its statute states that

1.
Daudet, L., *Souvenirs des milieux littéraires, politiques, artistiques et médicaux*, Chapter II, Paris, Robert Laffont, "Bouquins" collection, 1992, p. 171.

2.
See Martin Du Gard, R., *Les Thibault*, Gallimard, 1929.

the association's aim is "to promote the legal and social right to have control over one's own self, one's body and one's life in an independent, responsible manner [and] to choose freely how to terminate one's life so as to live it to the very end in the best possible manner" (Pohier, 1998). All the associations campaign for three things : the right not to suffer, the right to refuse unwanted life-prolonging treatment, and the right to voluntary euthanasia at the patient's request.

In the 1980s and 1990s, alongside these developments, the practice of illegal euthanasia was spreading. Death was caused by lytic cocktail or DLP, a combination of Dolosal, Largactyl and Phenergan, administered by intravenous injection, or by potassium injections. Certain doctors were actually to become specialists in the practice of euthanasia (or assisted suicide) at their patients' request. The best-known were Doctors Julius Hacketal in Germany, Peter Admiraal in the Netherlands, Jack Kevorkian in the United States and Léon Schwarzenberg in France.

Defining euthanasia

An ambiguous word

Littré's nineteenth-century dictionary of the French language defines "euthanasia" as "a good death, gentle death without suffering". The *Petit Larousse* dictionary gives the definition (translation) : "(Greek 'eu', well, and 'thanatos', death). Medical act of causing the death of an incurably ill patient to shorten suffering or ease dying, illegal in most countries." Another French dictionary, the *Robert,* dates the word's first appearance in French to 1771, with the meaning of "untroubled death". It defines euthanasia as (translation) : "gentle death without suffering, occurring naturally or through administration of analgesics or sedatives"; and alternatively as "the use of procedures to hasten or cause death in order to release an incurably ill patient from extreme suffering or on any ethical grounds".

In current usage, "euthanasia" has two conflicting meanings, that of "gentle death" and that of "deliberately caused death".

To avoid ambiguity the word is often qualified by an adjective. Thus:

- active (or direct) euthanasia signifies the act of causing death deliberately by administering a toxic substance which leads to death within a few minutes, but the term does not indicate whether the act is carried out at the patient's request;

- passive (or indirect) euthanasia, in one interpretation, means suspending all essential treatment with the intention of ending a dying person's suffering (it constitutes abandonment of the patient, contrary to Francis Bacon's recommendation and to Article 38 of the French Medical Association's Professional Code of Ethics); in a second interpretation it means suspending or rejecting unreasonable treatment (further chemotherapy, artificial means of respiration or an artificial kidney, for example); and in yet a third interpretation it is applied to death resulting from a necessary escalation in the dosage of sedatives administered to combat pain.

With or without the adjectives, the ambiguity persists.

In public debate the word "euthanasia" is used, confusingly, both in its etymological sense of "good" or "gentle" death and with its modern meaning of "deliberately caused death". The issue is presented as a choice between euthanasia (but which euthanasia?) and prolonging life artificially or unreasonably, or between euthanasia (again, which euthanasia?) and abandoning the patient. From time to time, opinion polls are conducted among the public and doctors, to find out if people wish "to die without suffering" or "to be helped to die". A survey by Ipsos for *Le Figaro* and France 3, in September 1998, posed the question thus: "If you had an incurable disease and were in extreme pain, would you wish to be helped to die?" The "Yes" vote accounted for 79% of responses and the categorical "No" vote 12%. An Ifop survey, commissioned by *Le Journal du Dimanche* and published on 15 April 2001, found that 38% of French people felt the law should now allow doctors to end the lives of patients with intolerable and incurable illnesses who requested death. The great majority of replies were positive, reflecting the fact that the questions could as easily be seen to relate to palliative care as to deliberately caused death. Yet the relationship of trust that must exist between a dying patient and his or her doctor would seem to require that we opt for a single meaning of the word "euthanasia", preferably an exact and unambiguous one.[1]

Five possible courses of action at the end of life : an analysis in the light of the French Medical Association's Professional Code of Ethics

We cannot hope to define euthanasia without first considering briefly five possible therapeutic approaches with incurably ill, dying patients.

These are :

1. administration of analgesics in progressive doses that may cause earlier death ;

2. restriction or non-use of active treatment or resuscitation ;

3. withdrawal of life support systems (such as artificial kidneys or artificial respiration) ;

4. helping the patient to commit suicide or assisted suicide ;

5. injection of a lethal substance.[2]

Approach 1 : death following administration of analgesics in progressively increasing doses, in order to relieve intolerable pain, is not wilfully caused, although the risk is known. It does not constitute euthanasia.

Approaches 2 and 3 involve not prolonging life artificially, in accordance with the patient's express wishes – if he or she is conscious – at the request of the patient's guardian or designated representative if the patient has lost the power of expression :

> *Article L 1111-6, Law No. 2002-303 of 4 March 2002 on the rights of the sick and the quality of the health care system*

> Any person of adult years may appoint a representative, who may be a family member, close relation or the attending physician, who is to be consulted if that person is unable to express his or her wishes or to receive the necessary information for that purpose. The appointment must be made in writing. It may be revoked at any time. If the patient so wishes, the representative

1.
See Aumonier, Beignier and Letellier, 2001, p. 8.

2.
Op. cit., p. 48.

may accompany him or her and may be present at medical consultations in order to help the patient take decisions.

Article L 1111-4, Law No. 2002-303 of 4 March 2002

If the patient is incapable of expressing his or her wishes, no procedure or examination may be carried out, unless in an emergency or where there is no alternative, except on the instructions of the representative appointed under Article L 1111-6, the patient's family or, failing those, a close relation.

Decisions not to undertake unreasonable treatment or treatments are in accordance with :

the French Medical Association's Professional Code of Ethics (1995), Article 37 :

"In all circumstances, doctors must attempt to alleviate their patients' suffering, support them emotionally and avoid any unreasonable insistence on investigations or treatments."

Recommendation 1418 of the Parliamentary Assembly of the Council of Europe, of 25 June 1999 :

"artificial prolongation of the dying process by [...] using disproportionate medical measures" is listed as one of the factors that today threatens "fundamental rights deriving from the dignity of the terminally ill or dying person".

Article L 1111-4, Law No. 2002-303 of 4 March 2002 :

"The doctor must respect the person's wishes, having informed him or her of the consequences of the choice to be made. If the person's wish to refuse or discontinue a form of treatment places his or her life in danger, the doctor must do everything possible to persuade the person to accept essential care."

Pope John Paul II's declaration of 25 March 1995 :[1]

"[...] one can in conscience refuse forms of treatment that would only secure a precarious and burdensome prolongation of life, so long as the normal care due to the sick person in similar cases is not interrupted."

1.
Evangelium vitae, encyclical of 25 March 1995.

The decision to restrict or discontinue any form or forms of treatment must be taken calmly, clearly and collectively ; it does not constitute a cessation of care or an abandonment,

Article 38 of the French Medical Association Professional Code of Ethics requiring that patients continue to be cared for and supported until the very end. If all these conditions are fulfilled, such a step in no way constitutes euthanasia because the intention is to respect the natural process of death.

Approaches 4 and 5 are of a quite different nature. Helping people to commit suicide, or assisted suicide, is illegal in most countries (except Switzerland and the state of Oregon in the United States of America). Injection of a lethal substance constitutes causing death, which is illegal in most countries except the Netherlands, Belgium and the state of Oregon.

According to the ADMD, Libre Pensée and Belgium's free-thinking "libre examen" movement, however, there is a fundamental continuity between the five approaches which, in their view, are all forms of euthanasia; whereas the associations promoting palliative care (for example, SFAP and JALMALV) and all religious authorities (except certain branches of Protestantism) take the opposite view.

A single meaning for "euthanasia": death caused deliberately

The definition we propose of **euthanasia is an action or omission with the primary intent of bringing about a patient's death in order to end his or her suffering.** This definition offers a straightforward criterion of conscience: euthanasia is an inflicted, as opposed to a natural, death.[1]

Euthanasia as thus defined is prohibited in the Preamble and Article 1 of the Universal Declaration of Human Rights and in the French Civil Code. Doctors are not allowed to perform it: the Hippocratic Oath includes the pledge "I will neither give a deadly drug to anybody who asked for it, nor will I make a suggestion to this effect", and Article 38 of the French Medical Association's Professional Code of Ethics states that doctors "must care for and support the dying patient right to the end, ensuring, by means of appropriate treatment and care, the quality of the life that is ending, preserving the patient's dignity and comforting those close to him or her. They do not have the right to cause death deliberately."

1.
See Aumonier, Beignier and Letellier, 2001, p. 51.

We recommend avoiding any other use of the word "euthanasia", whether in its etymological sense of "good death" or in the sense of passive euthanasia, in order to end confusion and misunderstandings.

Bibliography

Abiven, M., Chardot, C. and Fresco, R., *Euthanasie. Alternatives et controverses,* Paris, Presses de la Renaissance, 2000.

Ariès, P., *Essais sur l'histoire de la mort en Occident,* Paris, Le Seuil, *1959. (Western attitudes towards death,* London, Marion Boyars, 1976.)

Aumonier N., Beignier, B. and Letellier, P., *L'Euthanasie,* Paris, PUF, Que sais-je No. 3595, 2001.

Bacon, F., *The advancement of learning,* Book II (1605), J.M. Dent and Sons Ltd, 1973.

Bacon, F., "Instauratio Magna" (The great instauration), I, IV, 2 (1623), in Montague, B. (ed. and translator), *The works,* 3 vols., Philadelphia, Parry & MacMillan, 1854.

Carrel, A., *L'Homme, cet inconnu,* Plon, 1935, Le Livre de poche No. 445, 1975. (*Men, the unknown,* Hamish Hamilton, 1936.)

Chaunu, P., *La Mort à Paris (XVIe – XVIIe – XVIIIe siècles),* Fayard, 1978.

Lecourt, D. (ed.), *La Fin de la vie : qui en décide ?,* Paris, PUF, Diderot, 1996.

Mill, J.S., *Utilitarianism* (1863), J.M. Dent and Sons Ltd, 1972.

Pohier, J., *La Mort opportune. Les Droits des vivants sur la fin de leur vie,* Paris, Le Seuil, 1998.

Richet, C., *La Sélection humaine,* Paris, Felix Alcan, 1919.

Associations

ADMD (Association pour le Droit à Mourir dans la Dignité)
103 rue La Fayette, F-75010 Paris
Telephone : +33 (0) 1 42 85 12 83 ; email : admd@club-internet.fr

JALMALV (Jusqu'à la Mort Accompagner la Vie)
4 *bis* rue Hector-Berlioz, F-38000 Grenoble
Telephone : +33 (0) 4 76 51 08 51
132 rue du Faubourg Saint-Denis, F-75010 Paris
Telephone : +33 (0) 1 40 35 17 42 ; email : jalmalv@club-internet.fr

SFAP (Société Française d'Accompagnement et de Soins Palliatifs)
110 avenue Émile-Zola, F-75015 Paris
Telephone : +33 (0) 1 45 75 43 86

Euthanasia
and ethics

The contemporary advocacy of euthanasia

by Jean-Paul Harpes

We no longer die as our ancestors did and, in particular, we no longer perceive death as they perceived it. Advances in medicine, the increasingly technical nature of treatments, the fact that hardly any of us nowadays die at home with our families, and the development of palliative care have all radically altered the way that we now encounter death. The way that we perceive death has altered just as radically, if not more so, reflecting changes in our perception of the world and of ourselves, and in the values and standards by which we live, as well as certain social practices that have developed as a result of these changes.

How we die today

Advances in medicine and health have considerably delayed our rendezvous with death. Whereas 200 years ago only 8% of the population reached the age of 75, 58% nowadays live longer.[1] But while medical progress has increased life expectancy, it has also significantly lengthened fatal illnesses. The wait for death can now be interminable and hard to endure, particularly as the increasingly arduous nature of many treatments can gradually erode quality of life, despite periods of remission. And because of advances in medicine the elderly and senescent see the end approaching much longer. In a nutshell, we take longer to die nowadays, and while dying probably now involves less physical pain, it is not without mental suffering.

Further, while it is true that our significantly greater life expectancy allows us to shut out thoughts of mortality for much longer, the sudden onset of a fatal condition after many years of health can create great vulnerability. Young people to whom the idea of death has been quite foreign and who then develop Aids or another incurable disease will probably be even more vulnerable than others. Patients with incurable

1.
See Pohier, Jacques, *La mort opportune*, Paris Seuil,1998, p. 19.

conditions are also much better informed nowadays about what is happening to them. Even when doctors adopt a careful, gradual approach to telling patients that they have a fatal condition, the process of absorbing and adjusting to the bitter truth is highly painful.

General use of hospitalisation, the mushroom growth of nursing homes and the introduction and spread of palliative care (while much too slow in some countries, due to budgetary constraints) have all transformed the way that we now experience illness, aging and death, and our perception of death. On the one hand, care has improved significantly. In most cases, palliative treatments free the patient from fearful anticipation of a painful death. On the other, people with serious illnesses must resign themselves to long periods in hospital, and elderly people who have lost their independence end their days in nursing homes. The practice of systematic hospitalisation (an inevitable development) and the (equally inevitable) growth of the nursing-home sector have meant that old and sick people are transplanted into an environment that – despite the often impressive devotion of doctors and carers – is impersonal and lacking in warmth. Moreover, in 2-3% of cases, palliative care is ineffective or not effective enough. Physical suffering has not yet been eliminated – and nor has the fear of it. The dread of suffocating in the night which people with neuro-muscular degeneration experience can be unbearable. At the same time, absence of pain – and even the assurance that there will be no pain – cannot shield patients from despair or simply a sense of emptiness and futility. Old people ending their days in a nursing home may look back on the more intense relationships they once had with their families, and even on family quarrels, as aspects of a lost paradise. Too often their links with family have been all but broken. The inevitability of death may become an obsession in the empty days of a life where not much happens any more. This probably goes some way to explaining the high incidence of suicide among old people, and particularly old men. In the United States, the suicide rate among the over-65s rose by 25% between 1981 and 1986.

Our perception of death has been altered not only by the new medical environment but also by changes in our picture of the world and of ourselves and changes in the rules we live by. Because, in terms of ideas and norms, our perceptions of life and the end of life have evolved significantly, and are still evolving, our perception of death is different from that of previous generations.[1]

Attitudes to death have been affected by the increasing erosion of religious faith. Few of us retain absolute faith in an all-powerful God, creating and sustaining life. People facing death today tend to be thrown back on themselves and respond to the absence of God either with resignation or with indifference or defiance. The image of a world guided by a reassuring sense of purpose faded long ago.

Hand in hand with the decline in religious and metaphysical certainties, at least since the Enlightenment, has gone a developing consciousness – which is stronger than ever today – of individual autonomy. Individuals now aspire to shape their own future, to realise their conception of the right way to live. Although recognition of the patient's right to self-determination, and demand from patients for a degree of autonomy (a thing we allow young people and people with mental disabilities) are entirely consistent with these changing norms, they are relatively recent.[2] One aspect of the change has been a shift, albeit gradual, away from the traditional paternalism of the medical profession and towards doctor-patient dialogue, and the practice now is to inform patients prudently, with due allowance for the often difficult process of coming to terms with the truth. Having come through that process, patients are capable of giving informed consent and can be involved in choices as to treatment. They are in a position to co-decide what final road to take.

A further consideration is that our secular societies have not only spawned powerful demand for individual autonomy, but are also generally influenced by the ideal of the active, fulfilled, fit, healthy life, the ideal of prolonging youth and efficiency into our advanced years. From that perspective, the certainty of death, even without physical pain, is (or can be) hard to bear. People – or at least many of them – experience the frailty that comes with age, the dependence and the absence of horizons as marks of degeneration. If people with incurable illnesses, or

1.
Of course we have to recognise that perceptions in our society, in terms of culture and norms, are complex and confused, and that there is no such thing as a common set of ideas, values and rules. Multiculturalism, in contemporary societies, begins inside the individual's head.

2.
See the Council of Europe Convention on Human Rights and Biomedicine, known as the Oviedo Convention, European Treaty Series No. 164.

old people at the end of their days, see their situation in these terms, they may well – as suffering intensifies – come to prefer death to a life that either has nothing left to offer or is of such poor quality that it seems to them to be worse than death.

Insistence on autonomy in the face of death, and fear of a greatly diminished life, are reflected in the growing tendency for people in good health to draw up living wills specifying the types of treatment they would or would not wish to receive if they one day found themselves incapable of expressing their own wishes. The interest in living wills has to be interpreted, on the one hand, in the context of various very real dangers : road accidents, plane crashes, heart attacks or strokes brought on by overwork. On the other hand, and most importantly, it needs interpreting in the light of the overall perception of life and death that characterises our society.

What we have done so far is highlight at least some of the expectations and values informing the way that terminally ill patients, patients in dialogue with their doctors, very old people and people afraid of being caught off guard by death tend to perceive and shape the ends of their lives. From an external perspective, the perspective of those who witness patients' final suffering, compassion – which, however we see it, is one of the most widely shared values in our society – is a big factor in what we regard as a good death. It is also true that, from their own internal perspective, those who are in pain expect to encounter a basic level of compassion.

Perceptions of death and particularly of death as a release (or what others see as a release) are influenced, too, by actual practice and current law as regards actively assisting death, both in our own countries and in other countries. Europe generally is beginning to be aware of legislation and practice in the Netherlands, of the new Belgian legislation and of the fact that there are countries, notably Switzerland, which permit assisted suicide. Perceptions of death are already being coloured by these new laws, whether we regard them as liberating or ominous. The existence of organisations campaigning for the right to die with dignity is undoubtedly another factor that has helped to shape perceptions of death in very many countries.

The meaning of advocacy of euthanasia in our society

Exploring what advocacy of euthanasia means in our society, or societies, entails asking at least two questions. Firstly, what does the (active and insistent) euthanasia lobby signify or signal? Dictionary definitions of the word "signify" include "stand as a sign for" and it is this sense that we shall take as a starting point. What combinations of fact and circumstance, rules and aspirations does advocacy of euthanasia reflect in our society?

On the other hand, the significance of this advocacy is not confined to social and normative factors. Open in its approach, it is also explicit in its message, which, in our plural societies, is interpreted in more than one way. The second aspect of its significance, in and for our societies, is the many different ways in which the message is interpreted and read.

What does advocacy of euthanasia in our society signify or express?

At the risk of some repetition, it may be useful at this point to go over the ground from a fresh angle. Obviously, cultural changes in our society are, at least in some respects, at the root of contemporary euthanasia advocacy – they are part of its "significance". In this context, a set of new norms, or of new combinations of them, is particularly significant.

Contemporary advocacy of euthanasia is indicative, first and foremost, of a negative reality: the fact that certain religious, metaphysical and normative barriers to acceptance of euthanasia have crumbled.

On the one hand, very few of us nowadays acknowledge God as the sole master of life and believe that never in any circumstances is it permissible to end life. Interestingly, in the first few centuries of Christianity this position was not universally shared, as some modern religious writers have been quick to point out.[1]

Even fewer of us still consider that the world is set on a clear and purposeful course, that life has an inherent goal and that

1.
See Wils, J.-P., *Sterben. Zur Ethik der Euthanasie*, Paderborn, Schöningh, 1999, Chapter 4 of which includes a very useful outline history of euthanasia.

any interference with human life would conflict with the objective purpose that governs us all.

And while there is little disagreement in our societies about the very high value placed on life, we rarely ascribe to it an absolute or unconditional value. The value of life can be set in the scales like any other value and alongside other values. Moreover, the right to life, recognised in numerous international declarations, conventions and covenants, does not imply an obligation to live imposable on anyone who does not wish to live.

The second thing that contemporary advocacy of euthanasia points to is the combined influence of three norms or expectations which occupy a special place in our society.

The first of these is freedom and individual autonomy. This is a core ingredient of both political culture and ethical culture in a liberal society. Not only do individuals, at a profound level, see it as such, but as a society we also accord at least some autonomy to groups who would never have been granted it in the past. In terms of norms, recognition of people with mental disabilities as having partial autonomy is something new. Interestingly, people with mental disabilities account for a significant proportion of those who, in the final stages of illness, wish to die.

In a society pursuing the ideal of an active and fulfilled life, suffering and dependence are equated with shameful decline. Modern individuals, who want to shape their own lives, demand (or at least tend to demand) the right not to suffer such decline. Doctors, who now have a new partnership-based relationship with their patients, are bound to take that into account. Their sense of what is right impels doctors to observe patient autonomy no less than to alleviate physical decline.

Our society (and, in particular, our sense of what is fitting in dealing with bioethical matters) is driven not only by insistence on autonomy and revolt against the indignities of physical decline but also by an imperative of compassion for the sick. The doctor cannot accept a patient's decline, especially when accompanied by degrading physical pain – and this has always been so. But while doctors today have very powerful means of tackling pain, sometimes these are not enough. In

those rare and extreme cases, society acknowledges that practitioners have a right and a duty to alleviate suffering by progressively increasing the dosage of painkillers, even at the risk
of shortening the patient's life. But where is the boundary
between alleviating suffering and allowing someone to die?
Through compassion, doctors may cross the boundary and
many, indeed, feel duty bound to cross it. Medical compassion,
coupled with the patient's expectation of it, is probably the
root factor (or core "signified") of the euthanasia lobby. The
doctor may feel that patients who have ceased suffering but no
longer wish to live are an equally deserving case. "I don't want
to wake up again," such patients will say every morning at a
certain stage of their illness. It is the doctor who can give them
peaceful release.

Changing attitudes, wider acceptance of assisted death, the
sustained efforts of certain organisations, and new laws in
some countries – inasmuch as they form part of our society's
cultural horizon – are also part of the underlying social significance of contemporary euthanasia advocacy.

The social message of advocacy of euthanasia; alternative messages; the significance of the debate in our society

We have agreed that a second aspect of the euthanasia lobby's
significance in, and for, our societies is the range of ways in
which its message is interpreted and read.

Our societies are complex and multicultural in various
respects. Because multiculturalism begins inside the individual's head, there is no single social meaning to the justification
of euthanasia. Rather, societally, we have an infinite number of
complementary reactions to it.

None the less, it will be useful, even if somewhat artificial, to
begin by reconstructing what might be seen as the typical
message of contemporary advocacies of euthanasia which put
forward sets of legal proposals to decriminalise assistance with
death. In the eyes of those who are pushing for this (or something very similar), it is the lobby's (real) social point. At the
same time we shall reconstruct the typical message of those
who resist those proposals, regarding them as being the least

desirable social message. From their perspective, the real meaning of contemporary advocacy of euthanasia (or at least of that type of advocacy) is that society and its standards are on a dangerous course. Third and last, we will describe an intermediate approach.

The message of those who want voluntary euthanasia decriminalised,[1] and the social significance, as they see it, of permitting voluntary euthanasia under very strict conditions

The main components of this message are as follows.

Ethical acceptance of euthanasia in certain forms and decriminalisation of voluntary euthanasia (under very strict conditions) are a way round an impasse for society and its rule-making function. They would allow society to distance itself from a set of ancestral values that are no longer relevant in terms of social norms, and at the same time they have a liberating potential. They represent an adjustment of bioethical theory, practice and legislation to reflect our society's real feelings about what should and should not be allowed.

They amount to an acknowledgment by society of patients' autonomy in the final stages of terminal illness, and particularly of the "ultimate liberty". This has ceased to be regarded as sinful.

By removing what has been real inconsistency between practice and rules, acceptance of euthanasia and decriminalisation of voluntary euthanasia (under very strict and strictly monitored conditions) would put an end to cover-ups, hypocrisy and dishonesty.

By bringing much-needed transparency into relations between doctors, patients and families, they would help to reduce the risk of abuses.

Why, according to those who oppose decriminalisation of euthanasia, this message sets society on a dangerous course,[2] and what opponents see as the social significance of advocacy of euthanasia

Decriminalisation of euthanasia is, according to its opponents, dangerous in at least three respects.

1.
See, for example, De Closets, F., *La Dernière liberté*, Paris, Fayard, 2001, although the author's arguments do not exactly mirror the first type of message presented here.

2.
See, in this connection, views recently expressed by Jean-François Mattei, the French Minister for Health, the Family and Handicapped Persons. The message as set out here is inspired by, though not directly modelled on, his position.

Even if tightly limited and subject to rigorous conditions, decriminalisation would put the very basis of our society at risk. The rule that no one may dispose of human life must be absolute. Deliberately causing death must remain illegal. Any decriminalisation of procedures that bring about death would open the door to abuses. Fundamentally, there is no guarantee that the interests of families, carers or hospitals would not, on occasion, take precedence over those of patients.

Supporting a sick person in an extreme situation represents an existential challenge. It is not the type of challenge to which there can be a legal or technical answer.

It is wrong to claim dominion over life, by virtue of technology, from the cradle to the grave. Just like overzealous use of technology to create life, the desire for mastery of death involves a degree of hubris that virtually invites abuses.

The best way to respond to patients' physical and psychological pain in the final stages of illness is to step up the development of palliative care facilities, not to decriminalise voluntary euthanasia. There is a danger of decriminalisation impeding the spread of palliative care.

A third way : the social significance of a moderate approach

The third way borrows various elements from the first two approaches (with adjustments), while distancing itself from others.

In extreme situations, doctors (and their teams) are bound to deal with the physical suffering of terminally ill patients which, in rare cases, is not relieved, or is only very partially relieved, by the drugs available. They also cannot ignore a patient's clear and lucidly expressed wish to die, even if the suffering is essentially or entirely in the mind. Confronted by existential challenges in extreme situations, doctors (aided by their teams) and patients alone should decide, in all conscience, what course to take.

From this point of view, legislation is not appropriate. Indeed, it is probably unreasonable to seek a generally applicable legislative response to an existential challenge.

In short, the first position is that arguing for and decriminalising voluntary euthanasia are liberating steps that mark an ethical adjustment to a changed perspective, in turn requiring adjustment of the law to reflect present norms and actual practice. The second, opposing, position is that decriminalising euthanasia would inevitably be a dangerous step, implying major risks for society and calling into question the dignity of the sick. The third, intermediate, position is that, in such a sensitive context, the best response is a human one which takes account of extreme existential circumstances and accepts the possible consequences of making an agonising choice. Surely it is this position that represents victory for humanity, good sense and prudence?

The debate about dignity

by Göran Hermerén

Chilly wind sharp as a razor blade
House on fire, debts unpaid
Gonna stand at the window, gonna ask the maid
Have you seen dignity?
[...]
So many roads, so much at stake
So many dead ends, I'm at the edge of the lake
Sometimes I wonder what it's gonna take
To find dignity

Bob Dylan

By and large, the debate on euthanasia is difficult and emotional. Value-loaded terms are often used to describe the different positions ("pro choice" versus "pro life"; "respect for human dignity" versus "respect for the right to die with dignity"). A great deal is required to make a person change his or her view – regardless of whether that person is for or against euthanasia. Moreover, there are good reasons both for and against euthanasia – something that both critics and advocates of euthanasia sometimes are reluctant to acknowledge.

Definitions and types

The same event or action can often be described in several ways. A basic idea is that if a doctor had not omitted or performed a certain action, the patient would not have died at a certain time but later. It is obviously possible to say then that the patient died of the basic disease from which he or she suffered. But the time of death can be influenced by what the doctor chooses to do – or not to do. So in that sense, the person died at the particular time due to the intervention of the doctor.

Anyway, focus is not here on the moment of death (if indeed such a moment can be identified) but rather on the process of dying. Needless to say, the duration of this process in terms of minutes, hours and days can vary. This point will not be repeated below, though it is relevant also for a discussion of the main arguments for and against euthanasia, which is then not considered an end in itself but as a possible way to achieve the right to die with dignity.

Even if the concept of euthanasia is vague, it is important to distinguish between at least two types of euthanasia, namely :

- **voluntary euthanasia:** to help to die at the request of a patient ;

- **non-voluntary or involuntary euthanasia:** other forms of mercy killing, including mercy killing of infants born with grave malformations who could expect only a short life filled with misery and suffering, mercy killing of senile and demented patients suffering from cancer, muscle atrophy or ALS in the final stage, if the patients have not earlier expressed any request for help to die and cannot be assured a dignified and (reasonably) painless death.

The main reason for this distinction is obviously that the second category does not meet the requirement that what the doctor does – or refrains from doing – in order to shorten the life of a patient is done at the request of this patient. In these cases, the patient is unable to make such a request. Even if the patient were able to do so, the patient would not be able to understand that the intervention – or lack of intervention – by the doctor would shorten his or her life.

It will be important to keep this distinction in mind when we consider the ethical reasons for euthanasia. The principle of autonomy, the right to self-determination, the obligation we have to respect other people and similar ideas are often invoked to justify euthanasia. But it is easy to see that such reasons will only have some force as support of voluntary euthanasia. If, on ethical grounds, we want to argue for other forms of mercy killing, we will have to appeal to different principles and reasons.

Even if the distinction between the two types of euthanasia is important for the reasons just mentioned, it should be stressed that a number of different problems may arise when, in particular cases, we have to decide whether the particular conditions for euthanasia are satisfied or not. For example, how do we know that a request for help to die really expresses what the patient wants – rather than something else, such as a desire for more attention, better care, more time or a wish not to be a burden to society or to close relatives?

Two related general problems

The problem is often stated in terms of rights in the literature on the subject (for example, Nowell-Smith, 1987). But it may be an advantage to avoid the controversies over the existence and basis of rights and start the inventory of problems not by asking if there is a right to die with dignity but in a more open way.

Thus, leaving the issue of whether there exists a right to die with dignity open for the time being, a basic moral problem can preliminarily be stated in the following way: Are there situations in health care such that euthanasia (in the sense delimited here) is ethically justifiable? If the answer is yes, one could then go on to give examples of such situations, examine how common or uncommon they are, and discuss how they should be handled.

An interesting variant of the basic problem could be obtained by rephrasing the question above as follows: Are there situations in health care such that one ought not to criticise a doctor who in these situations would perform euthanasia? There is a small but not insignificant difference between these two ways of putting the problem.

How big the difference is depends on whether it is taken for granted that (1) what is not expressly ethically acceptable is ethically wrong, or (2) what is not ethically wrong is ethically acceptable. In other words, is there a domain of actions which we might call "ethically indifferent", and how is this domain related to the other categories?

In discussing whether there are reasons to praise or blame someone for an action performed or omitted by that person, it is reasonable to consider the situation of the agent, what that person knew about the situation, what his or her aims and motives were, what efforts had been made to obtain information about the alternatives and their consequences, and so forth. An action or an omission can be wrong, given certain ethical points of view (utilitarian, deontological, contractual, etc.). But it does not necessarily follow that one ought to blame the person who performed (or did not perform) that action. I shall refer below to the latter problem as the problem of justifiable criticism.

Problems at different levels

There may also be good reasons to separate problems at different levels from each other. The individual moral problem concerns what is right or wrong for a particular doctor to do in a certain situation. On the other hand, the institutional policy problem concerns whether the health care system as an institution ought to have and implement a general policy on this question.

The reason for the distinction between these problems is that it is possible to argue without contradicting oneself that each situation is specific, and in fact so specific that general rules cause more harm than good. Therefore, the decision should be left to the good judgment or discretion of the individual doctor. If guidelines are to be made, they should be stated and revised by the professional organisations rather than by politicians, health care boards or lawyers.

Relevant factors in the situations that may have an impact on the decision include the nature of the incurable disease, how close the end is, whether and to what extent a dignified death can be assured. Other relevant factors are to what extent adequate alleviation of the pain of the patient can be offered, the wishes expressed by the patient and the extent to which it is reasonable to interpret this wish as a genuine expression of what the patient wants, rather than as an expression of a temporary depression or something else, and perhaps also the wishes and beliefs of the family.

If the institutional policy problem is answered in the positive, it is natural – in the attempt to state general conditions or guidelines – to consider factors of the sort mentioned above. They are all somewhat vague, and different individuals may differ as to whether they think they are met. Therefore, it is possible and perhaps also desirable to consider various safeguards. For example, in the Netherlands, two doctors should independently of each other arrive at the same conclusion, or, as has been proposed by Nielsen (1998), ethics committees operating at a regional health board level are to approve legal euthanasia fitting within careful guidelines.

Openness – To what extent?

Then there is another family of moral problems concerning openness and transparency. Should one try to hide the fact that euthanasia is practised, if this is the case, or should this be generally known or acknowledged openly? Who should in both these cases have access to information about what is going on and the possibility – as well as, perhaps, the obligation – to review it?

It could be the case that euthanasia (in the sense delimited here) is practised and ought to be practised. But it does not necessarily follow that this practice should be discussed openly and be generally known, because this could create too much anxiety and distress, and undermine the trust between doctors and patients. These decisions should be left to the profession, with little or no openness and transparency. Such views, which I do not share (Hermerén, 1996), have been expressed more than once.

Also here there are several versions. According to one version, it ought to be known to everyone, or at least generally known in a particular country, if euthanasia is practised in that country. According to a more restrictive view, only those who are more or less directly involved in the actual cases ought to know – and are entitled to be informed. This means that the information is limited to the patient, the staff caring for the patient and, of course, the relatives.

Documentation – How?

If the issues discussed in the previous section can be referred to as the problem of openness, there is a related but rather more specific issue: the problem of documentation. If euthanasia in one form or other is practised, should this be documented? And if so, how and why? Clearly one form of documentation or other would be desirable in order not only to facilitate studies but also, and more importantly, to check that the conditions in the guidelines have been followed and to make enforcement possible.

The legal situation, and the standard medical practice, may vary from country to country. So let us begin by looking at some of the main options. They include:

– indirect documentation, stating what doses of which drugs were administered as well as what was not done at certain moments of the patient's time at the hospital;

– direct documentation, stating what doses were administered, etc., as above, and, in addition, the reasons for them.

Indirect documentation in the sense indicated above seems to be both legally required and standard medical practice in most countries. Confidence and trust in the health care system is based on the assumption that what is done is indeed done for the good of the patient, and that no secret practice takes place. If a patient or his or her relatives wants to find out what has happened, for instance, they could get information about the diagnostic tests and doses used.

A complication with direct documentation might be that the reasons or purposes might be complex – several reasons could be present at the same time – and that they could also be described in more ways than one. Let us suppose that certain reasons or purposes are considered to be morally acceptable (such as to alleviate suffering), others more dubious and still others morally not acceptable (such as, at least in certain countries, to shorten the life of a patient actively), then there could be a temptation to refer only to the ones that are considered to be acceptable. If this is done, we would not know for certain that other reasons did not play a part, nor the extent to which they did play a part.

If there are good reasons for allowing euthanasia (in one sense or another) and to answer some of the problems indicated above in the affirmative, the reasons for this could also be stated openly. Trying to cover up a practice for which there are good reasons, if indeed there are good reasons for it, will in the long run do more harm than good. So my own view is this: if euthanasia is ethically acceptable, this should also be generally known. The same holds true if euthanasia is practised.

Decisions on ethical issues are based on premises of different kinds, and the case of euthanasia is no exception. Facts and empirical assumptions need to be checked, and norms and values – including assumptions about the goals of medicine and the role of the doctor – need to be clarified.

Empirical problems

In this context, reliable empirical information is needed in order to arrive at stable and well-founded conclusions. But it is clear that in the debate so far empirical assumptions, for which there is as yet little evidence, abound.

For instance, how common are such requests? Suppose they are more common in certain countries than in others. How is this to be explained? And how are such requests to be interpreted? What a person says that he or she wants is not always identical to what that person wants. In particular, the praxes and attitudes of different involved and concerned groups need to be studied. Obviously, medical doctors are one of these groups. But there are also several other groups, whose attitudes and views are relevant and ought to be studied.

Thus, what we need to know is not only if and to what extent euthanasia in one form or another is practised in a particular country, we also need to know more about the attitudes and beliefs of various involved and concerned groups, which are all rather heterogeneous. In particular, we need to know their views on what I have called above the general basic moral problem, the problem of justifiable criticism, the institutional policy problem, the problem of openness and the problem of documentation – and perhaps also a number of other issues.

The main difficulty with empirical studies in this area is that the key terms are notoriously vague and unclear. Attempts to clarify current practice are often vitiated by uncertainty as to whether the person who constructed the survey and the person answering the survey have understood the key terms in the same way. The same holds true for attempts to identify attitudes to normative alternatives. The way the question is phrased can introduce a bias in the study which is difficult to control and to correct (Nilstun et al., 2000).

Anyway, it is necessary to underline that such empirical studies will not solve the problems. They would do so only on certain assumptions, which are obviously untenable. We would then need to take for granted that the attitude of the group studied is also the correct attitude – in that case, we could conclude what ought to be the case from a study of what is the case. But nevertheless empirical surveys can provide an important part of the information needed for a constructive dialogue on euthanasia.

Euthanasia and autonomy

Let us now turn to the normative issues and the basic values involved. In principle, there are two different main reasons for euthanasia. The first main argument is based on some version of the principle of autonomy, the right to self-determination, the obligation we have to respect other people and similar ideas. The second main argument – of which there also are several more specific versions – is based on the principle of non-maleficence and the principle of beneficence, that is to say, the requirement not to harm, and to do good by preventing and alleviating pain and suffering.

These principles can obviously be combined (Haan, 2002). But they will have somewhat different force, depending on what type of euthanasia is discussed, as mentioned above. These forms of euthanasia ought therefore to be discussed separately. The principle of autonomy – and its limits – is the natural point of departure when reasons for euthanasia at the request of a patient are looked for, especially if the discussion concerns what above was called the basic moral problem. What follows from the request or the obligation to respect the patient's will? According to some people, this is the only relevant consideration, and they let it decide the issue.

It should be noted that the emphasis on patient autonomy has increased both in medical research and in health care since the second world war, and that this emphasis is particularly strong in countries with liberal, individualistic political traditions, such as the Netherlands, the United Kingdom and the United States. The role of doctors in Japan, for instance, has traditionally been paternalistic, and the family has been more important than the individual. But there are signs that this may be changing, and that more people now wish that their own decisions would receive a greater amount of respect, particularly in situations involving death with dignity and euthanasia, according to a questionnaire reported by Hayashi et al. (2000).

But the principle of autonomy is not only respected to a varying extent in different parts of the world. It can also be interpreted in several different ways. If this is so, there is not just one principle of autonomy (Hermerén, 1994). Who is the subject whose will is to be respected? And how is a person defined in relation to others? Already the poet John Donne said long ago that no man is an island, and this is a point often stressed by social psychologists. Moreover, what does "respect" mean in this context? Listen to, consider carefully or heed and follow – or any intermediary steps? (Runeson et al., 2000)

Moreover, and more importantly, the autonomy of the patient needs to be balanced against the autonomy of other groups, in particular the autonomy of the doctors and the health care staff. Nobody should have to take part in euthanasia against his or her will. Suppose that the institutional policy problem – should the health care system as an institution have and implement a general policy on this question? – is answered in the affirmative. This then seems to require a clause of conscience (so that conscientious objectors can survive in the system) to the effect that a doctor who does not want to take part in this practice can remit a patient to another doctor. Such a clause would not be unique: similar clauses already exist in several countries in other areas.

Thus we have to consider the limits of autonomy: the obligation to respect one person's autonomy can be limited if what that person wants clashes with what another person wants. On the assumption that autonomy is decisive, we have to consider the autonomy of everyone involved. But sometimes one person's autonomy can be respected only at the price of not (fully) respecting somebody else's autonomy. Then there is a clash between these obligations.

Finally, and equally importantly, is the fact that autonomy needs to be balanced against other legitimate norms and values. This is the hard normative issue. Which other values are relevant, what is the ranking order between them – and how (and by whom) is this decided? This is a problem I will return to below. Then there is a clash between autonomy and other values.

Euthanasia, promoting good and preventing harm

The other main normative reason for euthanasia is that we have an obligation to do well, prevent harm and diminish suffering. But this reason is somewhat vague and ambiguous already because our concern may be directed at several of the stakeholders involved, such as the patient, his or her relatives, doctors, the health care staff, as well as other groups in society.

What is good for one of these stakeholders may not be good for others. What is good in the short term may be bad in the long term, and conversely. Moreover, there is the possibility that what is presented as a concern for the well – being of the patient may also be due to a concern for the well-being of the doctor or the health care staff. The situation of the relatives and the doctor is different in several ways. For one thing, the relatives may experience such a situation once or twice in their life, whereas the doctor may have to face it quite often if euthanasia is practised; thus, the emotional and ethical stress as well as the risk of blunting may well be different.

To put this point somewhat differently, decision-making at the end of life can be tough and exhausting. The actions performed or omitted by a doctor can be explained and supported by appealing to concern for present and future patients, who should not be worried unnecessarily. But this does not exclude that behind all this there is also concern for the doctor's own well-being, the well-being of colleagues and other health care staff.

An important aspect of the problem of respect for human dignity versus the right to die with dignity is that values are embedded in a cultural context. Therefore, this context needs to be made explicit, especially in multicultural societies. For instance, Lo (1999) stresses interesting similarities and differences between contemporary Western and ancient Confucian perspectives on death with dignity.

People may find it easier to agree on what is harmful and what should be avoided than on what is good and should be promoted. But even in the case of harm there are important cultural differences that should be taken into account. The complication there is that not only what is good for one of the parties involved may be bad for another, but also that the parties involved may have rather different views as to what is good and bad.

Euthanasia and consistency

Consistency is one of the virtues of moral life. Even if we cannot always agree on what the basic values are, we can often agree on the need to be consistent. If that requirement is given up, it will be difficult to anticipate and predict what others will do and value.

The application of this requirement to the present problems is rather conspicuous. The right to self-determination is important in a number of health care situations. Let us suppose that it is taken for granted that the wishes expressed by a patient ought to be respected in a number of situations but not when an incurably ill person requires euthanasia to ensure a dignified and (as far as possible) painless death. Then one should be able to point out some ethically relevant difference between these situations. If that is not possible, it will be inconsistent to treat the latter wishes differently from the others.

Another application of the requirement of consistency can be outlined as follows. Suppose first that there are doctors who themselves want to be able to receive help if they are incurably ill, the end is near, no adequate pain relief is available, and so forth. Suppose next that the number of these doctors is larger than the number of doctors who are prepared to give such help to their colleagues and others. Suppose finally that the golden rule is accepted : "Thou shalt do to others,[1] etc." Without criticising either the golden rule *per se* or those doctors who

1.
Matthew vii.12.

want to receive help but are not prepared to give help, it is then possible to argue that people are inconsistent if they want to accept the golden rule and are willing to receive but not to give similar help to others as they want themselves.

Dignity debated

Dignity is often invoked by advocates as well as critics of euthanasia : respect for human dignity is put against the right to die with dignity. Here, underlying ideologies clash, as mentioned above.

They can be described somewhat superficially as : sanctity of life versus quality of life, or the autonomy of the patient versus the sanctity of life. In one of these ideologies, life is a gift and not something for humans to take or finish. In the other, death is brought about to avoid or prevent a degrading existence. But what does "dignity" mean more precisely in this context? It is a difficult and elusive notion.

Besides, as stressed by Engelhardt (1998), the traditional Christian focus concerning dying is on repentance, not on dignity. The goal of a traditional Christian death is forgiveness and union with God. Viewed in that context, the contemporary focus on dignity in death and dying represents a clash between different cultures in a more or less secularised world.

Article 1 of the Council of Europe Convention on Human Rights and Biomedicine (the Oviedo Convention)[1] states that :

> "Parties to this convention shall protect the dignity and identity of all human beings and guarantee everyone, without discrimination, respect for their integrity and other rights and fundamental freedoms with regard to the application of biology and medicine."

However, there is neither here nor in the explanatory memorandum to this convention any precise definition of dignity and integrity, nor any precise statement when human life begins. This is not because the working party drafting the convention could not see the need for such a clarification – but because we realised the difficulties in finding agreement on them.

1.
See the Council of Europe Convention on Human Rights and Biomedicine, (Oviedo Convention) European Treaty Series No. 164.

Clearly, the expression "the right to die with dignity" can be interpreted in several ways, for instance, "the right to die without pain and suffering" or "the right to die with (maintained) respect for one's autonomy". In the first case, dignity-related reasons may be regarded as a special case of beneficence-related reasons. In the second case, they may be regarded as a special case of autonomy-related reasons.

If "dignity" is interpreted in terms of "integrity" (wholeness), we will obtain a new and different interpretation of the respect and the right mentioned in the dilemma, since the concept of integrity is neither identical to the concept of autonomy nor to the concepts of pain and suffering. New interpretations are then possible, depending on whether we think primarily of the physical integrity (wholeness) of the body, the identity and wholeness of the mind and the body, or of the mind in particular, all of which can be manipulated, undermined and destroyed in different ways.

But the expression "the right to die with dignity" can also be interpreted in a more general way, as "the right to die with a certain quality of life". The latter expression can then be operationalised in several ways. For example, as suggested by Bolmsjö (2002), a patient's physical dignity is violated if a patient dies naked and in pain ; the medical dignity is violated if the patient suffers from unbearable pain and further treatment is futile ; and a patient's mental dignity is violated if the beliefs and attitudes of the patient are not treated with respect.

Thus, a way around some of these conceptual problems might be to leave the precise definition of dignity open and first identify some generally agreed on obstacles for dignity, and then secondly see what could be done.

Is autonomy an end in itself? Or a means to some other end? Or both? What about consistency, beneficence and non-maleficence? Are they ends in themselves or means to other ends? In the latter case, what are the grounds for believing in the empirical assumption : if autonomy (consistency, non-maleficence, etc.) is granted or achieved, death and dying will be more dignified?

Economy and euthanasia

It is important to underline the danger of relating euthanasia at the request of a patient to controversies of a financial nature. The focus of the debate should be on humanitarian and ethical aspects of care at the end of life. A welfare society worth its name should afford to help terminally ill people requesting a dignified and, if possible, painless end of life.

In other words, it would be wrong to support or argue for euthanasia on the grounds that introducing and allowing such a practice will save money for the health care system. Sometimes it costs more, sometimes less, to provide people with the help they need and want. But such economic arguments have no place in a serious debate on the ethical aspects of euthanasia at the request of a patient.

Why? Such a discussion should take as its starting point some ideas about the goals of medicine and health care. These goals may include curing diseases, and if a cure is not possible, alleviating pain, and if that is not possible, comforting those whose wounds cannot be healed – or some variations on these ideas (Hastings Center, 1996). But these goals do not include saving money for the taxpayers.

This point can also be put as follows: if euthanasia is not ethically acceptable, it should not be allowed, even if the health care system would save money in that way. And if euthanasia is ethically acceptable, and even highly desirable, it should be allowed, even if it would make health care more expensive.

If indeed euthanasia is ethically acceptable, we will have to face a debate on setting priorities between different possible ways of allocating resources. The time and money spent on euthanasia will have to be compared to what we would get spending this time and money on other ethically acceptable and highly desirable interventions. This is in my view the only relevant place for economic arguments in this context.

What do the reasons show?

So far I have identified a number of autonomy-related, beneficence-related, consistency-related and dignity-related reasons for euthanasia. (The term "related" is used because it is possible to distinguish between several different reasons under each heading, related to the key concept.) What do these reasons show? Do they help to solve or illuminate the various problems identified before in a clear and convincing way?

The extent to which they may do so depends on several circumstances. First, it will depend on what the answer to these problems is taken to be. The questions outlined above in the first part of this paper can be stated as follows:

– Are there situations when euthanasia in the sense discussed here can be justified?

– Should an individual doctor who in a particular situation practices euthanasia be criticised?

– Should health care as an institution adopt and implement a policy regarding euthanasia?

– Should it be generally known in society at large (or at least by the relatives and health care staff involved) that euthanasia is practised?

– Should interventions with the aim of shortening the life of a patient be documented?

These questions can be answered by "yes, always", "yes, sometimes", "yes, but only under certain conditions" and "no, never". The force of the reasons identified above will depend on which of these general positions we are arguing for (or against).

Secondly, there can be good and strong reasons for euthanasia, but they do not necessarily show that euthanasia should be allowed or legalised – if there are better or stronger reasons against euthanasia. The possibility of undesirable social consequences of allowing or legalising euthanasia has been mentioned many times in the debate during the last decades. Such consequences may include encouragement of non-voluntary and even involuntary euthanasia, unconscious coercion of the terminally ill to request euthanasia, undermining the relation of trust between doctor and patient, and slowing down improvement of palliative care.

Thirdly, the evaluation of how undesirable such consequences are and thus of the force of these reasons will depend on a number of general and tacit premises. These premises need to be made explicit if we want transparency and openness. For example, they may include:

–   visions of the good life and the good death and dying, visions which philosophers from the days of Socrates, Aristotle and the Stoics to the present have tried to elaborate on;

–   more or less humanistic, technological and biological views of man, which are culturally conditioned and which are not chosen in the way a person chooses a particular dress for a social occasion.

Can these visions and views be proved? They cannot, in my view. But it is possible to argue for or against them, for instance, by pointing out – appealing to historical examples – what the consequences may be if they are adhered to and applied in different kinds of situations.

But sooner or later one will reach bedrock, a final point beyond which one cannot venture. But this does not mean that the position taken is arbitrary. There are unproven points of departure for all lines of argument, even in mathematics and the natural sciences.

Weighing up risks

In a way it could be said that the key issue in the debate on respect for life and human dignity versus the right to die with dignity is about weighing up risks. There is an obvious risk that some patients today will not be assured a dignified and painless death. Clearly, we – and particularly medical doctors and nurses – have an obligation to try to reduce their number as much as possible. But if this is not done? Or if this is not possible?

If euthanasia is introduced in order to reduce these risks, we may open the door for other risks – which those who oppose euthanasia do not hesitate to emphasise. These other risks include medical risks. As stressed by Lossignol (2002), numerous medications may induce death at supratherapeutic doses but few are effective in ensuring an end of life without suffering, though there are effective ways of providing easy and gentle death. But more importantly there are probably social risks, such as risks for misuse, as well as the risk that terminally ill patients and handicapped people will feel a pressure on them to ask for euthanasia in order not to be a burden to their relatives or to society.

Obviously, we then have to face a number of hard questions, dealing with both quantitative and qualitative aspects of risk assessment and risk management. Which of these risks are most serious? How do we weigh a certain but perhaps small risk against an uncertain but perhaps bigger risk? To live is always to take certain risks. Which risks ought to be accepted in order to avoid other risks? If the problem is stated in this way, it will also be easier to avoid painting a picture in black and white. The advantage, in other words, is that it will then be obvious that the problem is complex and that there is no simple and satisfactory solution from all points of view.

Reasons to reconsider one's point of view for a constructive debate

Conditions under which those who have taken a position on euthanasia might wish to reconsider their point of view:

1. Can alleviation of pain be so effective that incurably ill patients at the end of life receive what they consider to be adequate pain relief? In that case, one important reason for euthanasia will disappear.

2. Can the existential needs of incurably ill patients at the end of life be met so effectively that they can receive what they consider to be adequate help? In that case, another important reason for euthanasia will vanish.

3. Will palliative care in general develop in such a way that most patients will experience what they consider to be a dignified death? In that case, still another important reason for euthanasia will disappear.

4. Will the efforts currently made to improve palliative care stop or slow down if euthanasia is allowed? In that case, the conclusion is not that euthanasia – as in 1 to 3 above – is unnecessary, but rather that euthanasia is not desirable, perhaps even dangerous. This may also be the case if the questions below are answered in the affirmative.

5. Is there a risk that indications will change so that euthanasia, if allowed and practised, will be applied to individuals who have not asked for it, or who have asked for euthanasia because of temporary depression or external pressure? Is there, in other words, a risk that the distinction between voluntary and involuntary (as well as non-voluntary) euthanasia will not be maintained?

6. Are the conditions (risk of misuse, safety measures, openness and transparency, system of family doctors, traditions and prevailing attitudes) so different in two countries that what is ethically acceptable in one country would not be ethically acceptable in another?

The answer to these and similar questions will need to be based on empirical studies, which will then play a central role in the debate. Therefore, it is essential to insist on high-quality studies. This applies not only to the methods of selection, the way questions are phrased, the rate of non-response, and so forth, but also to the definitions, methods and assumptions on which the studies are based – they should be stated explicitly and examined critically. Moreover, these six points indicate some areas in which special protection of the vulnerable is needed if euthanasia is allowed in one form or another.

References

Bolmsjö, I.Å., *Existential issues in palliative care,* Lund, Department of Medical Ethics, 2002.

Engelhardt, H.T., "Physician-assisted suicide reconsidered : dying as a Christian in a post-Christian age", *Christian Bioethics,* 4(2), August 1998, pp. 143-167.

Haan de, J., "The ethics of euthanasia : advocates' perspectives", *Bioethics,* 16(2), April 2002, pp. 154-172.

Hastings Center, "The goals of medicine. Setting new priorities", *Hastings Center Report,* special supplement, November/December 1996.

Hayashi, M., Hasui, C., Kitamura, F., Murakami, M., Takeuchi, M., Katoh, H. and Kitamura T., "Respecting autonomy in difficult medical settings : a questionnaire study", *Japanese Ethics and Behaviour,* 10(1), 2000, pp. 51-63.

Hermerén, G., "Informed consent from an ethical point of view", in Westerhäll, L. and Phillips, C. (eds.), *Patient's rights. Informed consent, access and equality,* Stockholm, Nerenius & Santérus, 1994, pp. 39-61.

Hermerén, G., "Den goda döden och sjukvården", *Läkartidningen,* 93(10), 6 March, pp. 869-870.

Lo, P.C., "Confucian ethic of death with dignity and its contemporary relevance", *Annual of the Society of Christian Ethics,* 19, 1999, pp. 313-333.

Lossignol, D., "Euthanasie : les implications pratiques", *Revue Médicale de Bruxelles,* 23(4), September 2002, pp. A267-272.

Nielsen, T.O., "Guidelines for legalized euthanasia in Canada : a proposal", *Annals (Royal College of Physicians and Surgeons of Canada),* 31(7), October 1998, pp. 314-318.

Nilstun, T., Melltorp, G. and Hermerén, G., "Surveys on attitudes to active euthanasia and the difficulty of drawing normative conclusions", *Scandinavian Journal of Public Health,* 28(2), June 2000, pp. 111-116.

Nowell-Smith, P., "Death by request as a right", *Euthanasia Revue,* 2(12), spring/summer 1987, pp. 80-95.

Runeson, I., Elander, G., Hermerén, G. and Kristensson-Hall-ström, I., "Children's consent to treatment : using a scale to assess degree of self-determination", *Journal of Paediatric Nursing,* 26(5), September/October 2000, pp. 455-458.

Other references

Abbot, F.V., Gray-Donald, K., Sewitch, M.J. et al., "The prevalence of pain in hospitalized patients and its resolution over six months", *Pain,* 50, 1992, pp. 15-28.

Ahvenainen, J. and Nilstun, T., "Debattörer i Läkartidningen oense med studenter om aktiv dödshjälp", *Läkartidningen,* 96(14), 1999, pp.1731-1734.

Beck-Friis, B. and Strang, P. (eds.), *Palliative medicine,* 2nd edition, Stockholm, Liber 1995, 1999.

Doyle, D., Hanks, G.W.C. and MacDonald, N. (eds.), *Oxford textbook of palliative medicine,* Oxford, Oxford University Press, 1994.

Evans, R.W., "How then should we die ? California's 'Death with Dignity' Act", *Medicinska Etika A Bioetika,* 7(1-2), spring 2000, pp. 3-319.

Hall, A.C., "To die with dignity : comparing physician-assisted suicide in the United States, Japan and the Netherlands", *Washington University Law Quarterly,* 74(3), Fall 1996, pp. 803-840.

Kampits, P., "Ethische Probleme um des Lebensende. Sterbebegleitung – Sterbehilfe", *Wiener Medizinische Wochenschrift,* 152(13-14), 2002, pp. 317-319.

Kuhse, H. (ed.), *Willing to listen, wanting to die,* Harmondsworth, Penguin, 1994.

Kuhse, H., *The sanctity-of-life doctrine in medicine : a critique,* Oxford, Clarendon Press, 1987.

Kuhse, H. and Singer, P., *Should the baby live? Problem of handicapped infants,* Aldershot, Gregg Revivals, 1994.

Sandman, L., *A good death. On the value of death and dying,* Göteborg, Acta Universitatis Gothoburgensis, Kompendiet, 2001.

Singer, P., "The legalisation of voluntary euthanasia in the Northern Territory", *Bioethics,* 9(5), 1995, pp. 419-436.

Singer, P., *Practical ethics,* 2nd edition, Cambridge, Cambridge University Press, 1993.

Van der Maas, P.J. et al., "Euthanasia and other medical decisions concerning the end of life", *Lancet,* 338, 1991, pp. 669-674.

Woods, E., "The right to die with dignity with the assistance of a physician : an Anglo, American and Australian international perspective", *ILSA Journal of International Law,* 4(2), spring 1998, pp. 817-834.

Evaluation of the arguments

by Nicolas Aumonier

What weight do words and arguments carry when we or a loved one are staring death in the face or dying in pain? If we had the certainty of a dignified, pain-free death and being able to determine the time and manner of our going, might not we be spared pointless anguish and degradation? Might not the genuine respect which we owe ourselves and others require some kind of stoical, medicalised control over our final moments, some form of euthanasia, either voluntary or presumed so, if we are unable to express our wishes? The sick or elderly who are faced with these questions, their families, their doctors, lawyers, politicians and the public – all seem caught between the twin traps of oversensitivity and undersensitivity, short-sighted emotion and impossible logicality. Put simply, the question with allowing euthanasia is whether euthanasia is murder or a final care measure. Getting the arguments and words right is the very least we owe people in unspeakable distress. We shall look first at the various positions before attempting to evaluate the arguments.

The two traditional positions

Two main, opposing positions emerge right from the definition stage. Where a patient is in terrible (and possibly end-of-life) pain, there are five possible options, in order of increasing ethical difficulty:

– to administer analgesics in doses capable of causing death;

– to restrict or suspend treatment or resuscitation;

– to withdraw artificial maintenance of life;

– to assist suicide;

– to inject a lethal substance.[1]

Advocates of palliative care see a radical difference between the first three options, which are care measures (combating pain and refraining from therapeutic overkill) and the last two, which involve a decision to terminate a life (assisting suicide

1.
See Aumonier, N., Beignier, B. and Letellier, P., L'Euthanasie, Paris, PUF, p. 48.

and premeditated homicide), whereas the advocates of a right to euthanasia argue that all five involve euthanasia, taking a passive form in the first three options and an active one in the last two, given that the care provider is well aware of what the outcome will be and goes ahead. The former base their position on conscious differentiation between the two effects, the one desired (alleviation of pain), the second undesired (death). The euthanasia camp regard that distinction as artificial in that what is actually done (whether giving of an injection or withdrawal of treatment) is precisely the same. What criteria are we to employ to decide between two positions which are not even in terminological agreement about the thing that one side wants prohibited, the other permitted?

The real issue with the five options is where we draw the line. Here, emphasising the actual action and refusing to make a distinction of conscious intention is unhelpful. Is it my intention to free a bed for another patient, to end a dying patient's unbearable sufferings (unbearable for whom – the patient, me or the family?), or to make the patient's pain more bearable without knowing precisely when death will supervene, and preserving as far as possible what life remains to the patient? It is only in terms of intention that we can distinguish between a lethal injection and a heavily sedative one. For purposes of drawing the line, the care provider needs a definition centred on differentiating between actual intentions. The classic definition of euthanasia as an act or omission primarily intended to bring about a patient's death so as to end their suffering provides a simple criterion: euthanasia is an inflicted death as opposed to a natural one. That is a definition that allows people to clarify their intentions. It is a liberating definition. Do intentional use of euthanasia and intentional non-use of euthanasia have equal justification?

How valid are the classic arguments?

Three concepts are commonly used in allowing or disallowing resort to euthanasia: consciousness, respect and universality. What validity do they have?

Consciousness and the dual-effect argument

The classic exposition of the dual-effect argument is to be found in Thomas Aquinas' *Summa theologiae*, in connexion with the permissibility of killing in self-defence:

> "Nothing hinders one act from having two effects, only one of which is intended, while the other is beside the intention. Now moral acts take their species according to what is intended, and not according to what is beside the intention, since this is accidental [...]. Accordingly the act of self-defence may have two effects: one is the saving of one's life, the other is the slaying of the aggressor. Therefore this act, since one's intention is to save one's own life, is not unlawful, seeing that it is natural to everything to keep itself in 'being' as far as possible. And yet, though proceeding from a good intention, an act may be rendered unlawful if it be out of proportion to the end. Wherefore if a man, in self-defence, use more than necessary violence, it will be unlawful; whereas if he repel force with moderation his defence will be lawful [...]. Nor is it necessary for salvation that a man omit the act of moderate self-defence in order to avoid killing the other man, since one is bound to take more care of one's own life than of another's."[1]

To be applicable the dual-effect argument involves very strict requirements. The act has to be good in itself, the ill-effect must not be willed, even if it is foreseen (to foresee is not to will), the ill-effect must not be used as the means of achieving the good effect, and nor must it be worse than the good effect. Lastly, there must be no other possible course of action. When we apply this reasoning to use of analgesics we can say that such use is unobjectionable in itself (unlike injection of a lethal substance), that death is foreseen (without precision) but not desired, that death is not the means of achieving absence of pain and that death is not worse than the desired absence of pain since the illness will result in death in any case. Lastly, having no other possible course of action consists here in not using dangerous analgesics if harmless ones are available. Thus seeking to assist someone at no point involves seeking to harm them. Seeking to alleviate pain at the risk of causing death is not at all the same thing as causing death in order to end pain.

1.
Second Part of the Second Part, Question 64, Article 7.

But use or not of the dual-effect argument depends on how much confidence we have in the concept of consciousness. For some writers, the dual-effect argument – like consciousness and interiority – is an illusion, a myth, a social invention. Either our ability to stand back from our actions is a dream which has no knowledge of its own very specific determinants and, being a dream, has no access to the real nature of actions ; or it is an ancestral memory of the blows and brandings with which our forefathers were physically taught the rules that their masters, who were the rule-makers, declared to be universal or necessary to the common good (which was of course the good of the rule-making class). In the case of euthanasia, that lack of confidence would seem to weigh less heavily in the balance than the risk of killing someone who may have requested death but does not necessarily desire it. To draw that distinction, consciousness is a convenient notion which, despite – or with – our obvious limitations, gives us some grasp of actuality and allows us to identify some kind of priorities in what we do. The dual-effect argument is one tool for measuring my intentions and the priorities which I set myself in my actions. It must, however, be acknowledged that the dual-effect argument has no validity for a Spinozist, for whom the concept of freedom is totally unmeaningful given (he would argue) that we are wholly determined and have no access to what it is that determines us.

Respect for what ?

If consciousness appears suspect, can we at least agree about respect ? Bioethical writings of a Kantian turn make considerable use of the word. It sometimes looks like a vague injunction involving some kind of very general goodwill. What precise meaning are we to ascribe to it ?

Respect for the human individual is an argument used by Leibnitz and Kant in two distinct, but very similar, forms. According to Leibnitz, to pass fair judgment one has to place oneself in other people's position.[1] That not only takes into account all individual standpoints but also fits them into the rational scheme devised by God, who alone confers existence on the best possible and mutually compatible combinations.

1.
New essays, I, II, 4, end.

There is nothing subjective or limited about this "real" standpoint. The truth which it reveals is a total truth which gives that standpoint universality. This concept of the universal depends not on belief in God but purely on belief in total human rationality, in an aggregate of what reason is capable of. In Kant's view the only way of avoiding a morality contaminated by the various sensitivities contained in the concept of happiness is to give it universal form. The rules governing our actions must be uncontradictably universalisable. Respect/obedience is supra-sensitive recognition of the moral law as an unconditional universal imperative. Whether the universal is a sum total of determining factors, as in Leibnitz, or an unconditional absolute, as in Kant, its perspective-widening function is identical: to overcome introversion and broaden our thinking so as to encompass all human beings. In the medical context of the final stages of human life, what scope does respect have? Is it universal or relative?

The care provider, concerned for the patient's well-being, may be led to draw a distinction between respect for the patient's wishes and respect for the patient's organism. Three possible situations then arise.

First situation: the patient, no longer wishing to live, or no longer wishing to live in the manner in which he or she is living, requests termination of life. They may ask to be provided with a substance which they can themselves take or inject (assisted suicide) or they may request action which only the care provider, given the patient's incapacity, can perform (euthanasia). In the vast majority of cases, such requests will cease if appropriate analgesic treatment is given. A very few people, however, will feel themselves to be nothing short of imprisoned if the right to end their lives is refused them. Existential revolt of this kind takes a utilitarian view of medicine as provision of services: one person with strong personal feelings is placing an obligation on another to act on those feelings. In actual fact no patient can legally compel a doctor to terminate their lives, given the illegality of murder. Even more importantly, the tacit medical contract[1] between doctor and patient requires that the doctor provide conscientious, attentive care

1.
The medical contract: the judgment of 20 May 1936 which the French Court of Cassation delivered in the Mercier case established the contractual nature of the legal relationship between doctor and patient, laying down the principle that "between doctor and client there is a genuine contract under which the doctor undertakes, if not (needless to say) to cure the patient – that has at no point been alleged – but to provide not just any care [...] but conscientious, attentive care which, other than in exceptional circumstances, is in accordance with the state of scientific knowledge".

in accordance with the state of scientific knowledge. Such care is intended to be for the patient's good.

But what if the patient takes a different view of what that good is – for it is the patient's body – and sees it not in terms of what is existent, or of his or her own body, or of what the political, emotional or family community regards as good, but in terms of what he or she regards as good at the particular time? Is that not the patient's right, and is there not an obligation on everyone to respect it? The classic objection is that undue pain, or ignorance of possible alleviations, may render the patient incapable of a fully informed judgment. Others, it is argued, know better than the patient. Medical paternalism of this kind is not without its difficulties either. In the case of a patient who wants to have done with it all, does good lie in maximising the length of life or in striking a proper balance between length and quality of life? But in the latter case, who is the judge of what the proper balance is? The family's inability to come to terms with death, or medical practitioners' hope that treatment, however drastic, can still save the patient, can open the door to therapeutic overkill that nobody wants. What criteria can we apply to avoid that?

There would appear to be three philosophical positions. The first is that there exists an absolute good, that it is to be ascertained in the individual case and that whatever action is taken by everyone involved must be consistent with it (this is the Aristotelian or Thomist school of thought). The second is that good is merely what I call whatever I desire : I view as good what I desire and as bad what I abhor (Spinoza). The third approach consists in deciding what is good by negotiation (see, for example, Tristan Engelhardt and the seeking of consensus in peaceable dispute-settlement).

The urgency of dealing with pain sometimes rules out negotiating an approach with everyone involved. A decision then still has to be taken, but according to what conception of good? If good is simply the name I give to whatever I desire, it means that the concept of good is as fluctuating, variable and physiologically conditioned as my desire itself. But the body, when sick, does not always know what is good for it – and death is irreversible. Someone who requests death, viewing it as what is good for them, cannot say with any certainty that they would not view it as bad a few minutes later if the ability to picture a future, or enjoyment of life, were restored to them.

In addition, if patients had the right to demand that the doctor end their lives at their lucid and repeated request the conflicting duties to provide care and take life would be inconsistent with the concept of a medical contract (under which patients renounce some of their freedom in order to receive care from better-informed persons whose care decisions are taken in terms of what they consider to be in the patient's general interests, which involve the patient's physical interests). If there were no generally accepted benchmark of what is good for the patient there could not be any valid contract, and all concept of social contracts would be endangered. But if we put ourselves in other people's place and ask ourselves whether everyone, in the individual doctor's place, could unobjection-ably take the same course of action as the doctor, and if the answer is yes, then we are once again on the firm ground we need. Desire for death therefore cannot take precedence over provision of care, and provision of care cannot be turned into ending of life. The ultimate respect is thus respect for a body. As a good applicable to an organism, this respect is basic to the concept of a medical contract. The ultimate good of the body cannot be left to the patient to decide. What we choose to regard as intolerable violence or as a prudent course of action may equally go under the name of social contract, social bond, fellow feeling or solidarity.

The second situation is where someone who is incapable of expressing present wishes has explicitly asked that previously expressed wishes, as set down in what is often termed a living will, be acted upon. So as not to be a burden on family, friends or the community, or to be spared a needlessly degrading end, or to be sure of not being used for clinical experiment, someone signs a statement that their life is to be curtailed in specified circumstances in which they are unable to restate their wishes. The problem is that we can have a change of mind and yet no longer be able to express it. In addition, there is no foreseeing what our precise wishes will be when we are dying – death as imagined when we have a future ahead of us is not at all the same thing as what someone experiences whose life expectancy is very limited. When it comes to it, a day longer, or even just an hour longer, may seem hugely important, indispensable for a peaceful end. Imagining one's death is not the same thing as living it. Nothing about our deaths is predictable. No living will or previously expressed wishes can retain validity when death approaches. No one could tie themselves to something so illusory or that could so absurdly turn into a trap. Respect for the individual must therefore take into account the possible multiplicity of the individual's wishes. Caution will always dictate that we prefer a perfectible situation (appropriate analgesic treatment or better human support) to an irremediable act (euthanasia).

The third situation is total absence of expressed wishes. Here, care providers would clearly be exceeding their role if they were to impute a desire for life – or death – to the patient entrusted to them.

In all cases respect, in practice, is respect not for someone's expressed wishes but for a body, not because the body is somehow sacred but because it is the first and last receptacle of the will to live which the living organism contains right through to life's end. Respect in practice has to be as wide in scope as possible, entailing respect for the body right to the end and constantly effective treatment with analgesics. That respect consists not in inflicting life on someone who does not want it but in trying to preserve the patient as far as possible from the imprisonment of pain so that the desire to die widens into a desire to live, which is a universal. Euthanasia and pain have equal capacity to imprison. Combating pain is more precautionary than doing away with life.

The universal

Can unbearable, all-invasive pain – a factor that no argument should overlook – make it legitimate to kill the body if that alone will overcome the pain ? To end suffering, is it sometimes necessary to end life ?

Logicians draw a distinction between the subject and what we can say about it (its predicates). If I say "Paul is in pain", the subject "Paul" is not reduced to its predicate "in pain". I can replace that predicate by another, such as "not in pain". But if I take away the subject "Paul", I can no longer attach any predicates to it, not even "not in pain", since the subject no longer exists. From the point of view of logic, it makes no sense to do away with Paul in order to do away with his pain. And if we entertain the possibility of a life after death such that Paul retains physical existence, the non-equivalence of the present life and what may only be a piece of wishful thinking to resign us to the void forces us to stick with logic and opt to end Paul's pain by means of appropriate treatment rather than by doing away with Paul. But can it not be argued that Paul's suffering is so inseparable from Paul himself that attacking the pain is impossible without attacking Paul, so that we must ignore logic and alleviate Paul's suffering by ending his life? No – for someone who is dead is also dead, as it were, to the choice between suffering and not suffering. To ignore logic on the pretext of exceptional suffering is to surrender to the suffering, to let the suffering take charge instead of the individual. Massive sedation will always be more respectful of the individual than a lethal injection. There seems to be no logical argument in favour of euthanasia.

Is there a third course of action?

In between rejecting euthanasia (as makes good logical and rational sense) and the strongly pro-euthanasia position, is there a third course that would not leave society torn between the pro and anti camps and which, without turning euthanasia into a right of the patient, would allow euthanasia to be used in certain circumstances? In other words, even though euthanasia is murder, may there be circumstances that make it legitimate? When all hope is lost, there are those who suggest,[1] not decriminalising euthanasia, but setting up a special tribunal to consider whether the care provider who administers euthanasia should be prosecuted.

Various provisions appear questionable. Firstly, to allow a third party to consent to the euthanasia of a close relative, as in the

1.
See: opinion delivered by France's National Consultative Committee on Ethics in Health and the Life Sciences (CCNE) on 27 January 2000; the Netherlands legalisation of euthanasia on 1 April 2002; and Belgium's legislation on the matter.

extended-consent model devised in connection with biomedical experiment,[1] is perhaps to make rather large assumptions about that person's disinterestedness (they may, after all, stand to inherit). Above all, there is a great difference between consenting to an, in principle, reversible clinical experiment (the patient can pull out of the experiment) and consenting on another person's behalf to the irreversibility of euthanasia. Secondly, by the time the matter is referred to the tribunal there is generally nothing more to be done. Nor is the tribunal a mechanism for debate. It confines itself to examining a fact, or possibly only recording it, which is unlikely to produce any finding as to what might constitute a minor or more serious breach of the law. Thirdly, being wholly dependent on what is or is not reported to it, the legal system cannot deal with what is deliberately hidden from it and thus is powerless to influence covert illegal practices. If the legislator's aim is to put an end to the previous hypocrisy of doing surreptitiously what was officially prohibited, then the attempt is doomed to failure : there will always be people who are prepared to disregard the law. More importantly, authorising assisted suicide and euthanasia in order to bring things out into the open may simply mean more illegalities going unpunished and the spread of formerly covert practices, with refuge being taken in presumed consent.

Even supposing these difficulties can be overcome by tightening up the provisions, there remains the basic question whether the law can create a right to break the law – a right, recognised by a tribunal, to be treated as an exception. If the rule of respect for the human individual ceases to be universal as soon as it runs into some practical difficulty, then arguably it completely ceases to operate, spelling an end to patients' trust in the medical profession, shortly followed by loss of public confidence in the social contract which governs social and political life. To base a right on some mere subjective (and, by definition, changeable) desire is to damage the universality of the law. Allowing euthanasia on compassionate grounds ends in eugenicist euthanasia of very seriously handicapped children going *de facto* unpunished.[2]

Surely the function of a statute, rule or directive is to call back into line those who might be tempted to take too large a view ?

1.
CCNE opinion of 27 January 2000.

2.
Henk Jochemsen estimates that the lives of some ninety handicapped children were terminated in the Netherlands in 1995 (Jochemsen, H., "Euthanasie. Leçon des Pays-Bas : la régulation est-elle opérante ?", *Laennec*, 48(6), October 2000, p. 7).

Confirmation of this is possibly to be found in the French tradition. Firstly, we need to clarify our use of the word "exception". In French law the *exception de procédure* is a procedural challenge to one's opponent's position. It does not constitute a substantive ground of defence. However, a jury in the assize court or the criminal court are at liberty, in France, to reclassify an offence, take motive into account and decide whether an offence should be prosecuted. Given, therefore, that it is already open to the legal system law to give consideration to special circumstances without necessarily passing adverse judgment, legislation introducing special rules on euthanasia is scarcely needed to introduce further flexibility. Or is case-law flexibility such a worry to some that they need a statute to absolve them of the need to exercise their own judgment? If some people, however few, regard euthanasia as murder, it is not possible to legalise it without, in their view, making murder legal, bringing down the entire legal edifice and excluding from the social contract everyone who persists in viewing euthanasia as a crime. Only conscience can be the judge of an exception, but allowing exceptions in principle risks undermining patients' confidence in doctors. Henk Jochemsen's conclusion (translation) is that "once euthanasia is officially approved and practised, it takes on a dynamic of its own which makes proper control difficult and tends to spread. That creates a situation that saps the foundations of the rule of law".[1] Making euthanasia a special case poses a serious risk to human rights.

Euthanasia in the strict sense would seem to be justifiable only by means of arguments which run counter to the concepts of equality before the law, the social contract and human rights. Making it legally possible seems pointless (proper sedation adapted to the individual case can now deal with all pain) and a danger to human rights. The final stages of our lives are our last opportunity to exercise our freedom. Instead of being thrown away in despairing attempts to have done with it all, they are to be valued as being the final stages of our humanity. To do away with them would be to reduce human beings to animals. It is not their unbearability that humanises us; rather it is we who must make their painfulness more humanly

1.
Ibid., p. 9

bearable, thereby becoming ourselves more human. The individual at the outposts of human experience, approaching, then encountering, the enigma of death – as every other individual has done or will do – will be united right to the end with doctors, family and friends, in a common respect for humanity and a shared – if at times paradoxical – love of the life being lived out.

Bibliography

Dictionnaire permanent bioéthique et biotechnologies, Paris, Editions Législatives. See "Euthanasie, acharnement thérapeutique et soins palliatifs".

Abiven, M., Chardot, C. and Fresco, R., *Euthanasie. Alternative et controverse,* Paris, Presses de la Renaissance, 2000.

Aurenche, S., *L'Euthanasie, la fin d'un tabou?* Paris, ESF, 1999.

Baird, R. and Rosenbaum, S.-E., (eds.), *Euthanasia: the moral issues,* New York, Prometheus Books, 1989.

Beignier, B., *Respect et protection du corps humain. La mort. Art. 16 à 16-12 du Code civil,* Fascicule 70, Juris Classeur, 1997.

Canto-Sperber, M., *Dictionnaire d'éthique et de philosophie morale,* Paris, PUF, 1996. Articles: "Euthanasie" (Goffi, J.-Y.), "Double effet" (Byrne, P.), "Eugénisme" (Morange, M.), "Vie et mort" (Fagot-Largeault, A.), "Nihilisme" (Saint-Sernin, B.) and "Casuistique" (Carraud, V. and Chaline, O.).

Hennezel de, M., *Nous ne nous sommes pas dit au revoir. La dimension humaine du débat sur l'euthanasie,* Paris, Robert Laffont, 2000.

Hocquard, A., *L'Euthanasie volontaire,* Paris, PUF, 1996.

Israël, L., *La Vie jusqu'au bout. Euthanasie et autres dérives,* Paris, Plon, 1993.

Kant, I., *Sur un prétendu droit de mentir par humanité,* 1797.

La Marne, P., *Ethiques de la fin de vie. Acharnement thérapeutique, euthanasie, soins palliatifs,* Paris, Ellipses, 1999.

Leguay, C., *Mourir dans la dignité. Quand un médecin dit oui,* Paris, Robert Laffont, 2000.

Maret, M., *L'Euthanasie. Altèrnative sociale et enjeux pour l'éthique chrétienne,* Paris, Saint-Augustin, 2000.

Pinckaers, S., *Ce qu'on ne peut jamais faire. La question des actes intrinsèquement mauvais. Histoire et discussion,* Fribourg (Switzerland), Editions Universitaires/Paris, Editions du Cerf, 1986, reprinted 1995.

Pohier, J., *La Mort opportune. Les Droits des vivants sur la fin de leur vie,* Paris, Le Seuil, 1998.

Rachels, J., *The end of life : euthanasia and morality,* Oxford, Oxford University Press, 1986.

Somerville, M., *Death talk : the case against euthanasia and physician-assisted suicide,* McGill-Queen's University Press, Montreal, 2001.

Tavernier, M., *Les Soins palliatifs,* Paris, PUF, Que sais-je, 2000.

Verspieren, P., *Face à celui qui meurt,* Paris, Desclée de Brouwer, 1984, reprinted 1999.

Zoller, E., *Grands arrêts de la Cour suprême des Etats-Unis,* Paris, PUF, 1997.

What is palliative care?

by Tony O'Brien

Traditionally, palliative care or hospice care was associated solely with the care offered to patients during the final stages of life. Indeed, access to palliative care services was often restricted to those patients suffering from advanced cancer, at a point in their disease when the prognosis was likely to be measured in days or weeks. Palliative care was sometimes described as "terminal care" or "care of the dying". This association with death and dying is perfectly understandable, yet it fails to appreciate the true scope and potential of palliative care. Whilst end-of-life care is an integral element of palliative care, it does not define our discipline. End-of-life care is a continuum of palliative care. Palliative care accepts the inevitably of death, yet focuses on maintaining the best possible quality of life for patients and their families. Palliative care is life affirming, and seeks to create the space in which patients are enabled and encouraged to live, truly live until the end of their natural life.

Notwithstanding the important role of palliative care at the end of life, it has much to offer selected patients and families at an early stage in the disease trajectory. Indeed, many patients will benefit from palliative care support from the moment of first diagnosis. Access to palliative care services should not be limited to those patients suffering from cancer or any other specific disease type or pathology. Consideration must also be given to the needs of those suffering from non-malignant diseases. Ultimately, all patients who require palliative care should be able to access such care at a time and in a setting consistent with their clinical needs and personal preferences.

Palliative care fully supports and endorses the ethical principles of non-maleficence (not to cause deliberate harm) and beneficence (to do the most positive good). Palliative care does not embrace any ideology that supports the intentional ending of a patient's life, with or without his or her consent, regardless of the underlying motive. Palliative care is concerned with creating the opportunity for persons to live their lives as fully as possible, for the entire duration of their natural life. In the context of palliative care services, we seek neither to prolong life unnaturally nor to end life prematurely. Rather, the focus is on measures that are life-enabling, life-enriching and life-affirming. Whilst recognising the reality of our shared mortality, every effort is made to enhance life and quality of life.

Definition of palliative care

Palliative care is a rapidly evolving and dynamic discipline that is interpreted and applied in a variety of styles and in a range of different settings. It is acknowledged that there is no one entirely satisfactory definition of palliative care. The term "palliative" derives from the Latin "pallium" meaning to mask or cloak. In the context of advancing disease, it is evident that when we cannot fundamentally reverse or even retard disease progression, then we have a duty of care to minimise or ameliorate the effects of the disease on the patient. This does not necessarily mean that we should abandon all disease-modifying treatments. The relative merits of all approaches to care, both disease-modifying and symptomatic (although even this division is entirely artificial), must be assessed on an individual basis and subject to regular review.

Referral to a palliative care service is sometimes interpreted as an implicit acknowledgement of the fact that "there is nothing more to be done". This is wrong ; it is wrong for all patients and it is wrong in all situations. There is always more to be done. Patients with advanced and progressive disease must not be abandoned, nor must they be made to feel as if they have been abandoned. Dr Michael Kearney highlighted the need for a basic attitudinal change when he wrote :

> "Patients with incurable disease must no longer be viewed as medical failures for whom nothing more can be done. They need palliative care, which does not mean a hand-holding, second-rate soft option, but treatment that most people will need at some point in their lives, and many from the time of diagnosis, demanding as much skill and commitment as is normally brought into preventing, investigating and curing illness."(Kearney, 1991)

In 1990, the WHO defined palliative care as the active, total care of patients whose disease is not responsive to curative treatment. Control of pain, of other symptoms, and of psychological, social and spiritual problems is paramount. The goal of palliative care is the achievement of the best possible quality of life for patients and their families (WHO, 1990).

The WHO definition is commendable to the extent that it is patient-focused, and recognises that each patient will be part of a greater social network or family. Even defining the concept of "family" may be difficult. Perhaps, it is advisable to include all those who are significant to the patient, as determined by the patient. This definition may or may not include blood relatives. Additionally, the WHO definition does seek to address the multifaceted nature of the human condition (holistic), and consequently recognises the important role that will be played by a variety of professional and family carers. It identifies the goal of palliative care as the best possible "quality of life" for the patient and family. The issue of quality of life requires further discussion and will be addressed later in this paper.

The major criticism of the WHO definition is its focus on the term "curative treatment". This element of the definition is unclear and open to misinterpretation. This focus on cure is unhelpful, as medical developments will often result in patients living with progressive illness for considerable periods of time. More recently, the WHO has redefined palliative care as follows:

> "Palliative care is an approach which improves quality of life of patients and their families facing the problems associated with life-threatening illness, through the prevention and relief of suffering by means of early identification and impeccable assessment and treatment of pain and other problems, physical, psychosocial and spiritual." (Sepulveda et al., 2002)

Palliative care

- provides relief from pain and other distressing symptoms;
- affirms life and regards dying as a normal process;
- intends neither to hasten or postpone death;
- integrates the psychological and spiritual aspects of patient care;

- offers a support system to help patients live as actively as possible until death;
- offers a support system to help the family cope during the patient's illness and in their own bereavement;
- uses a team approach to address the needs of patients and their families, including bereavement counselling, if indicated;
- will enhance quality of life, and may also positively influence the course of illness;
- is applicable early in the course of illness, in conjunction with other therapies that are intended to prolong life, such as chemotherapy or radiation therapy, and includes those investigations needed to better understand and manage distressing clinical complications.

Patient autonomy

Respect for patient autonomy is one of the most basic and fundamental rights governing the doctor-patient relationship. Health care professionals and ethicists generally agree that persons have the right to make their own decisions about health care issues. Competent and informed adults have an established legal right to reject medical advice, assessment or treatment, except in cases where this decision causes harm to others or conflicts with legislation.[1] The right to refuse screening, diagnostic procedures or treatment can be for reasons that are "rational, irrational or for no reason".[2]

In general, it is clear that persons may refuse medical treatment. However, health service providers are not necessarily obliged to provide services on demand. Individual health care providers will not offer treatments in a variety of circumstances for perfectly valid and legitimate reasons. For example, a physician will not offer a treatment or procedure that is not indicated, is futile or is dangerous. This matter is particularly relevant in the context of physician-assisted suicide. For some patients, the right to choose the manner and timing of their death is seen as the ultimate expression of patient autonomy. It may be argued that the decision to end one's life is a personal

1.
Advance statements about medical treatment, report of the British Medical Association, 1995.

2.
Per Lord Templeton in Sidaway v. Board of Governors of the Bethlem Royal Hospital and Maudsley Hospital, London, 1985 AC 871.

matter that does not impact on the rights of others. However, patient autonomy is not absolute. Health care professionals cannot accede to the specific wishes of one patient without reference to the wider societal implications of the action. The involvement of physicians in taking action intended to prematurely end the life of a patient has far-reaching negative consequences for society as a whole. The current safeguards applicable in most jurisdictions serve to protect the most needy and vulnerable in our society.

Quality of life

The single most important objective of all health care programmes is to offer individuals an optimal quality of life. This is true for all patients and in all circumstances, yet it is a source of considerable confusion and debate. Perhaps, the difficulty stems from the fact that there is a fundamental failure by many health care professionals to understand precisely what is meant by quality of life. For some, it may relate to physical or cognitive functioning. For others, it may be understood to mean the absence of physical or mental illness. However, quality of life is a much more complex phenomenon and it certainly cannot be measured by reference to a single variable.

Quality of life is totally subjective. Consequently, it is not possible for one individual, whether he or she is a health care professional or not, to make a reliable judgment on the quality of life of another. Researchers have attempted to measure quality of life by proxy ratings, with limited success (Seckler et al., 1999). More recent research data has demonstrated that patients with incurable advanced cancer are very good judges of their quality of life (Waldron et al., 1999). Quality of life is whatever an individual person determines it to be for himself or herself, and it relates to a particular point in time. The issue of time is important. As our circumstances change over time, we will define and redefine the most important elements of our lives that contribute to its quality. In the context of a rapidly progressive disease process, we may redefine our priorities frequently over a short period of time.

Calman has defined quality of life in cancer patients as the difference or the gap that exists at a particular point in time between the hopes and expectations of the individual and that individual's present experiences (Calman, 1984). In essence, this definition recognises that quality of life is subjective, multidimensional and dynamic in nature. We may seek to improve quality of life either by improving an individual's current reality, for example by alleviating distressing physical symptoms, and/or by helping individuals to adopt more realistic expectations. In practice, both approaches are usually employed concurrently.

This understanding of quality of life raises potential difficulties in the context of advance directives. In this situation, a person makes a judgment about preferred treatment options (usually treatment-limiting options) based on their projected assessment of their quality of life at some future date. Quality of life judgments are valid only when current. Advance directives require persons to catapult themselves forward in time, to a situation that they can scarcely imagine, and to make important treatment choices. In reality, it is very difficult to predict the choices that one might make at some future date. Essentially, as a result of life events and experiences, we quite literally become different people, with different expectations and different needs.

Quality of life is now recognised as an end point of secondary importance only to survival (Anon., 1986). Relatively little empirical research data exists on patients' judgments about how they view their own quality of life. Physicians are more decisive than patients in making end-of-life decisions (Danis, 1991). Yet, it is recognised that treatment decisions should be based on values, goals and preferences of patients (Orentlicher, 1992). All decisions made in relation to patient care should seek to ensure that individual quality of life is preserved and enhanced to the greatest possible extent.

Decision-making – Initiating treatment

The key clinical and ethical question that must be addressed on an individual basis is whether or not a particular intervention or treatment will serve the best interests of the patient. In other words, will this particular treatment enhance or detract from the patient's overall quality of life. On occasion, there might be some short-term disadvantage, but a treatment might be justified on the expectation of a more sustained benefit. Also, it might be determined that a particular intervention is more likely to cause harm than benefit. In the latter case, the particular treatment should not be offered. However, if having assessed all of the variables, it is decided that a particular treatment is indicated, it should be offered to the patient with appropriate explanations and discussion.

From a medical and ethical perspective, there are two questions that must be addressed when selecting appropriate therapies for patients with advanced disease. The first question is to establish what can be done; that is, what are the possible therapeutic options. The second and much more difficult question is concerned with the appropriateness of a specific intervention. The fact that something can be done does not necessarily mean that it should be done. The real skill in clinical medicine rests in deciding when it is appropriate to offer a treatment and when it should be withheld.

Commonly, the decision to initiate treatment will involve much deliberation and consultation. The patient's views are paramount, but in order for the patient to contribute to the decision-making process, he or she must be aware of the relevant facts. All decisions concerning individual health care issues must be discussed and agreed with each individual patient. In order to make such decisions, patients should receive all relevant information in a manner that is appropriate to their level of insight and understanding. Whilst patients have an undisputed right to receive all information relating to their disease process and therapeutic options, they are not obliged to do so. Health care professionals must be sensitive to the particular needs of each individual patient, in terms of the timing and extent to which they wish to hear bad news. Patients have a right to know and a right not to know; at least, they have a right not to be confronted with information that they are not seeking and that they patently do not wish to hear. Consequently, health care professionals must develop skills and strategies that will equip them to communicate effectively, honestly and compassionately with patients and their families.

Decision-making – Withholding and withdrawing treatment

The needs of patients with advanced and progressive disease will change and evolve over time. Whilst a particular intervention, for example nutritional support might have been entirely proper and appropriate at a point in time, it may become evident that to continue such a treatment is inappropriate or futile. The issues involved in withholding or withdrawing treatments are particularly difficult. The term "passive euthanasia" is sometimes applied to describe the situation whereby a potentially life-sustaining treatment is stopped or withdrawn. This is an unfortunate choice of language. For all patients, and at all stages of the disease process, it is necessary and proper to evaluate and re-evaluate the relative merits of all treatments. If it is determined that the adverse effects of a particular treatment outweigh any potential beneficial effects, then it should be withdrawn. This is particularly common in the context of fluid and nutritional support at the end of life.

Doyal and Wilsher have noted that "competent elderly patients have a legal and moral right to decide whether to receive life-sustaining treatment. Such treatment should not be withheld or withdrawn on the basis of a patient's age alone. Principles for making decisions about life-sustaining treatments in incompetent elderly patients can be defended and should exist as written guidelines" (Doyal et al., 1994). The authors propose a series of "justifiable conditions for non-treatment of incompetent patients". While such guidelines might be of help, it is important to remember that all decision-making must be individualised, and tailored to the unique set of circumstances affecting a unique individual at a specific point in time. In the nature of guidelines in general, there are often difficulties relating to definition and interpretation.

Ethically, we are informed by the principle of proportionality. We are advised that we are not obliged to subject patients to excessively burdensome or futile treatments. However, when considering the term "burdensome" it is important to recognise that this adjective is applied solely to the particular treatment that is under consideration and must not be applied to the life of the patient. It is clearly contrary to all principles of palliative care that we would base any medical decision on an assessment of the burdensome nature or otherwise of a human life.

Decision-making – Incompetent patient

The complex issues surrounding information exchange and decision-making will be evident. The situation becomes significantly more challenging when, for whatever reason, the specific patient is unable to contribute to the decision-making process. Again, the principles of non-maleficence, beneficence and proportionality will apply in an effort to achieve and maintain the best possible quality of life for each patient. The relative merits of all treatments, both current and potential, must be subject to regular, systematic review. The views of family and professional carers should be canvassed and opportunity should be created for discussion and explanation. Ultimately, the senior clinician with responsibility for patient care should make the decision on the appropriateness or otherwise of all therapies.

In essence, palliative care is primarily concerned with facilitating and enabling persons to live their life as fully as possible. It is focused on achieving and maintaining the best possible quality of life for each individual patient and their family, for the duration of their natural life. All available diagnostic and therapeutic strategies should be used appropriately, to achieve agreed objectives. Palliative care seeks at all times to respect the integrity, individuality and unique worth of each person regardless of their ability or functional status.

"You matter because you are you, and you matter all the days of your life."[1]

1.
Dame Cicely Saunders, founder of the first unit of palliative care at St Christopher's Hospice in London.

References

Anon., "Outcomes of cancer treatment for technology assessment and cancer treatment guidelines", *Journal of Clinical Oncology,* 1996, 14, pp. 671-679.

Calman, K.C., "Quality of life in cancer patients : an hypothesis", *Journal of Medical Ethics,* 10, 1984, pp.124-127.

Danis, M., Southerland, L.I., Garrett, J.M. et al., "A prospective study for advance directives for life-sustaining care", *New England Journal of Medicine,* 324, 1991, pp. 882-888.

Doyal, L. and Wilsher D., "Withholding and withdrawing life-sustaining treatment from elderly people : towards formal guidelines", *British Medical Journal,* 308, 1994, pp.1689-1692.

Kearney, M., "Palliative care in Ireland", *Journal of the Irish Colleges of Physicians and Surgeons,* 20(3), 1991, p. 170.

Orentlicher, D., "The illusion of patient choice in end-of-life decisions", 267, *JAMA,* 1992, p. 2101-2104.

Seckler, A.B., Meier, D.E., Mulvihill, M. and Paris B.E., "Substituted judgment : how accurate are proxy predictions ?", *Annals of Internal Medicine,* 115(2), 1991, pp. 92-98.

Sepulveda, M.C., Yoshida, A. and Ullrich, T., "Palliative care : WHO global perspective", *Journal of Pain and Symptom Management,* 24(2), 2002.

Waldron, D. et al., "Quality of life measurement in advanced cancer : assessing the individual", *Journal of Clinical Oncology,* vol. 11, November 1999, p. 3603-3611.

World Health Organisation, *Cancer pain relief and palliative care, report of a WHO expert committee,* Geneva, 1990.

Ending or extending life-sustaining treatment: ethics of the decision

by Georg Marckmann

The progress in biomedical technology has provided physicians with an ever increasing repertoire of life-sustaining interventions. The benefits of these modern techniques like cardiopulmonary resuscitation, mechanical ventilation, renal dialysis or artificial nutrition and hydration are uncontested in the treatment of acute critical illness. In other situations, however, the benefit for the patient may be questionable: in patients who are in a permanent vegetative state, for example, these interventions allow one to sustain life artificially for many years with little or no chance of recovery. In terminal illness, life-sustaining interventions may just prolong the dying process and thereby cause unnecessary distress to the patient. In general, physicians face the challenge to avoid two different types of errors (Lo, 1995):

– withholding a potentially beneficial treatment that the patient would want;

– imposing a treatment that is no longer beneficial or does not correspond to the patient's wishes. In these situations, physicians' obligation to sustain life conflicts with the obligations to relieve suffering and respect the informed choice of the patient.

Decisions about withholding or withdrawing life-sustaining treatment are not purely medical decisions, but rather involve value judgments about the relative benefits, risks and burdens of different interventions and the patient's expected quality of life. Consequently, decisions about life-sustaining interventions should be based on the patient's values and preferences. Competent and informed patients have the right to decide for themselves whether they want to continue or forgo life-sustaining treatment. However, decisions about life-sustaining interventions often have to be made when patients lack full decision-making capacity. Hence, they are closely linked to the problems of surrogate decision-making: how shall we decide for patients who are no longer able to decide for themselves? In my paper, I will discuss several ethical considerations that should be taken into account in decisions about ending or extending life-sustaining treatment.

Assessment of the medical situation: the problem of futile interventions

Any decision-making about life-prolonging treatments should start with a thorough assessment of the medical situation: sound ethical judgment requires accurate medical information (Lo, 1995). During the medical workup the following questions should be answered (McCullough and Ashton, 1994):

- What information do we have about the medical condition of the patient?
- What treatment options are available based on up-to-date clinical evidence (including withholding life support)?
- What are the expected benefits and burdens of each treatment option for the patient?

Controversies arise about the benefit of life-sustaining interventions if they just prolong the dying process of a terminally ill patient. In such situations, the interventions are frequently considered as pointless or futile. While most physicians agree that they have no obligation to offer futile interventions, there is a long-standing and still unresolved debate about what constitutes a futile intervention (Kopelman, 1995; Schneiderman et al., 1990; Tomlinson and Brody, 1990; Truog et al., 1992; Youngner, 1988).

Medical interventions are beneficial or futile only with regard to a certain goal of care. Claims about futility therefore involve value judgments about the appropriate goals of care, such as sustaining human life, relieving suffering, improving physical functioning or comforting the patient. While it is the physician's primary competence to decide which is the best medical means to achieve a certain goal, the goal of care itself must be determined by or at least together with the patient. Of course, physicians have an obligation to inform the patient about the goals that can be realised with different management strategies in a given medical situation.

Bernard Lo has suggested distinguishing between a strict and a loose definition of futility. In the strict sense, claims of futility are based on clinical judgment and therefore justify unilateral decisions by physicians to withhold or withdraw a treatment (Table 1).

Table 1: When does futility justify forgoing interventions?[1]
The intervention has no pathophysiologic rationale.
The intervention has already failed in the patient.
Maximal treatment is failing.
The intervention will not achieve the goals of care.

If the term "futility" is used in a looser sense, it involves value judgments about the goals and prospects of interventions (Table 2). For example, how small the likelihood of success must be to justify forgoing interventions cannot be determined by scientific evidence alone. Claims about the worth of different goals of care and judgments about the patient's quality of life are inherently subjective and therefore should be based on the specific values and preferences of the patient. In these cases, physicians should not make unilateral decisions to forgo life-sustaining interventions. Rather, they should involve patients or surrogates in a process of shared decision-making. If physicians unilaterally declare interventions as "futile" in this loose sense, value judgments may be masked as scientific expertise (Lo, 1995). Even more controversial are considerations about what prospective benefits for the patient justify spending the resources required. These decisions should be based on a societal consensus rather than on an individual physician's judgment.

Table 2: Loose definitions of futility[2]
The likelihood of success is very small.
No worthwhile goals of care can be achieved.
The patient's quality of life is unacceptable.
Prospective benefit is not worth the resources required.

Ending or extending life-sustaining treatment: the competent patient

The principle of respect for autonomy requires that patients have ultimate decision-making authority. Respecting patients' autonomous choices is especially important in decisions about life-sustaining treatments, because they are usually based on

1.
Lo, 1995, p. 73.
2.
Lo, 1995, pp. 75-76.

value judgments about the benefits, burdens and risks of different treatment options. Accordingly, any intervention should be authorised by the patient's informed consent. Beauchamp and Childress have specified seven elements that are implied by the concept of informed consent (Table 3).

Table 3: Elements of informed consent[1]
I. Threshold elements
1. Competence (to understand and decide)
2. Voluntariness (in deciding)
II. Information elements
3. Disclosure (of material information)
4. Recommendation (of a plan)
5. Understanding (of 3 and 4 above)
III. Consent elements
6. Decision (in favour of a plan)
7. Authorisation (of the chosen plan)

In decisions about life-sustaining treatments, patients should be well informed about their medical condition and the available treatment options. If withholding or withdrawing a life-prolonging intervention is an option, the physician should also discuss the available strategies for palliative and terminal care. Patients should be able to arrange the last stage of their life according to their individual preferences. Informed decisions require sufficient time to reflect and ask questions about the available treatment options. Patients should be encouraged to invite family members or other persons they trust to join the deliberation and support their decisions. If the patient has a chronic condition that is likely to progress in the near future, physicians should discuss future treatment options with the patient (see section below on advance care planning).

There is wide agreement that competent and informed patients have the right to refuse interventions even if the refusal results in serious harm or their death. This especially applies to end-of-life situations: patients should be given authority to decide for themselves about the benefits and burdens of prolonging life in terminal illness. If physicians are convinced that refusal

1.
Beauchamp and Childress, 2001.

will cause more harm than good to the patient, they may attempt respectful persuasion – a weak paternalism – and try to convince the patient that further extension of life will be in his or her best interests. However, physicians should never override the informed decision of a competent patient only because they believe it would be better for them (Lo, 1995).

Assessing decision-making capacity

Decisions about ending or extending life frequently have to be made for patients who – due to their illness – lack full decision-making capacity. Some patients may be completely incapable of making any decisions, while others may make decisions that contradict their best interests. In the latter case, there is an ethical conflict between physicians' obligation to respect patients' rights to decide for themselves (respect for autonomy) and the obligation to protect them from harmful consequences of their own choices (beneficence). Patients' decision-making capacity varies along a continuous range and there is no natural threshold for an adequate level of competence. However, a binary decision has to be made: either patients have adequate decision-making capacity and their choices should be respected, or they lack capacity to decide for themselves and their wishes may be ignored (Buchanan and Brock, 1990; Lo, 1995).

And things are even more complicated: competence may not only vary over time, but also with the particular decision to be made. Some authors therefore have suggested a sliding-scale approach to assess a person's competence for decision-making: "Because the appropriate level of competence properly required for a particular decision must be adjusted to the consequences of acting on that decision, no single standard of decision-making consequence is adequate."[1] According to this approach, a higher level of competence is required if the patient's decision will result in a worse risk/benefit balance than alternative recommended treatment options. Conversely, a lower level of decision-making capacity is required if the patient's choice will result in a better risk/benefit balance than other available alternatives. While this sliding-scale approach certainly has some appeal, its practical application might be problematic: it heavily depends on physicians' assessment of risks and benefits of medical interventions and therefore

1.
Buchanan and Brock, 1990, p. 52.

"might allow physicians to exercise inappropriate control over patients with whom they disagree".[1]

Other authors have suggested that patients are competent to decide about their medical treatment if they are able to give valid informed consent. "Patients or subjects are competent to make a decision if they have the capacity to understand the material information, to make a judgment about the information in light of their values, to intend a certain outcome, and to communicate freely their wishes to caregivers or investigators."[2] Making competent medical decisions requires several abilities that can serve as a clinical standard for the assessment of the patient's decision-making capacity (Table 4).

Table 4: Clinical standards for decision-making capacity[3]
The patient makes and communicates a choice.
The patient appreciates the following information:
– the medical situation and prognosis;
– the nature of the recommended care;
– alternative courses of care;
– the risks, benefits and consequences of each alternative.
The patient's decision is stable over time.
Decisions are consistent with the patient's values and goals.
Decisions do not result from delusions or hallucinations.

If the decision-making capacity varies over time or with the course of the illness, a careful reassessment of the patient's competence is advisable. Any treatment options that might improve the patient's competence should be taken into consideration. In addition, physicians should provide any assistance patients may need to reach and communicate a competent decision. In the following section I will discuss how decisions can be made for patients who lack full decision-making capacity.

Ending or extending life-sustaining treatment: patients who lack decision-making capacity

Surrogate decisions for patients who lack adequate decision-making capacity should be based – as far as possible – on the

1.
Lo, 1995, p. 83.

2.
Beauchamp and Childress, 2001, p. 71.

3.
Lo, 1995, p. 85.

patient's beliefs and values. Depending on how much is known about the patient's prior preferences, three general standards for surrogate decision-making may be applied (see Figure 1):

– pure autonomy;
– substituted judgment;
– the patient's best interests.[1]

If a patient has expressed his or her wishes about the use of life-sustaining interventions in an oral or written advance directive, these prior autonomous preferences should be respected (pure autonomy standard). If no prior autonomous judgments are available, surrogate decision-makers should make a decision based on the patient's values, beliefs and preferences: "What would the patient choose under these circumstances?" (substituted judgment standard). If little or nothing is known about the patient's health-related preferences, surrogates should decide according to the patient's best interests (best interests standard).

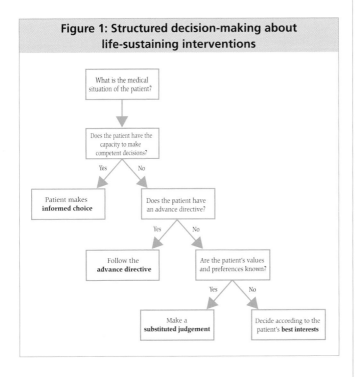

Figure 1: Structured decision-making about life-sustaining interventions

1.
Beauchamp and Childress, 2001, p. 99.

The pure autonomy standard: advance care planning

The pure autonomy standard applies if patients with impaired decision-making capacities have expressed their autonomous preferences when they were still competent. These advance directives can have the form of an oral statement or a written document. Patients can determine who should act as surrogate decision-maker or indicate what kind of interventions they would accept or refuse when they have lost decision-making capacity. Following advance directives respects patients' autonomy under circumstances in which they can no longer decide for themselves.

However, there are several concerns about the use of advance directives.[1] Because many patients with a chronic illness adapt to some extent to functional losses, it is difficult for them to anticipate what treatment options they will prefer at the time when they have actually developed the illness. In addition, advance directives may not exactly address the present clinical situation of the patient and therefore require a considerable amount of interpretation. Patients may also change their mind during the course of their illness. Sometimes, following the patient's advance directive may contradict the patient's best interests. In spite of these concerns, advance care planning remains the best available instrument to respect patient autonomy when patients have lost decision-making capacity. To be valid and clinically relevant, advance directives should be based on a thorough discussion about the use of life-sustaining interventions.

Advance care planning for patients with terminal illness should also include decisions regarding cardiopulmonary resuscitation (CPR) and artificial nutrition and hydration. If CPR is likely to be ineffective or will cause more harm than good to the patient, it might be appropriate to make an advance decision not to attempt resuscitation (Do-Not-Resuscitate Order). Whenever possible, patients should decide for themselves whether the expected benefits from a successful CPR outweigh the potential risks and burdens.

The substituted judgment standard

If no prior autonomous judgments of the patient are available, surrogate decision-makers must decide on behalf of the

1.
Lo, 1995, p. 95 *et seq.*

patient: What would the patient's choice be under the present circumstances? Substituted judgments should be based on the available information about the patient's values and preferences regarding the use of life-sustaining interventions. Consequently, surrogate decision-makers must be sufficiently familiar with the patient's prior beliefs and preferences. Family members or close friends should be consulted even if they do not formally act as surrogates. However, there are several concerns about substituted judgments that need special consideration.[1] Empirical studies suggest that proxy decision-makers frequently fail to identify patients' choices regarding life-sustaining interventions. Hence, we should always keep in mind that substituted judgments are inherently speculative: we do not really know what the patient would have decided in the present situation. The accuracy of substituted judgments can be improved if patients and surrogates explicitly discuss the patient's treatment preferences before decision-making capacity is impaired by the illness. There is also the danger that surrogates confound their own assessment of the situation with the patient's hypothetical choice. If only little is known about the patient's preferences, it might be more appropriate to admit that the decision is based on what the surrogate believes is best for the patient.

The best interests standard

If little or nothing is known about the patient's values and preferences regarding life-sustaining interventions, surrogate decision-makers should decide what they consider to be best for the patient. These decisions are guided by the ethical principle of beneficence: surrogates should maximise the benefit and minimise the harm for the patient. This requires a careful comparative assessment of the benefits and burdens of the available treatment strategies. Inescapably, this involves also an assessment of the patient's prospective quality of life. Such assessments, however, are inherently subjective and might be shaped by the proxies' specific preferences. In addition, healthy people tend to underestimate the quality of life, because many patients with chronic conditions have learned to live with the limitations of their illness and continue to enjoy life. Therefore, it is not surprising that surrogates may

1.
Lo, 1995, p. 109.

disagree over what is best for the patient. Unfortunately, the best interests standard is the last resort in deciding for incompetent patients. If nothing is known about the patient's prior preferences we have virtually no alternative to deciding what we consider best for the patient. However, we can try to reduce the arbitrariness in determining the best interests of the patient by involving several persons in the decisions : family members, physicians and other members of the health care team. Where there is substantial disagreement about the best interests of the patient, it might be helpful to consult a clinical ethics committee.

After withdrawal of life support: assuring appropriate end-of-life care

After a decision has been made to withdraw or withhold life-sustaining interventions, the dying patient should receive the same respect and compassionate care like any other patient. Patients and family members should be assured that forgoing life-sustaining interventions does not mean that nothing more can be done. Rather, the goal of care is changing from cure and recovery to palliation and relief of suffering. Physicians' primary concern should be to relieve symptoms, to control pain and distress, to improve functional status and to ameliorate emotional, religious and spiritual concerns. Any effort should be made to tailor the end-of-life care to the individual preferences of the patient, including the selection of a comfortable surrounding for receiving care. This requires a "structured deliberation" among patients, surrogates and physicians about the appropriate goals of care in the end-of-life situation (Emanuel, 1995).

Decisions about artificial nutrition and hydration are especially contested. For some people, nutrition and hydration are part of the basic care that never should be withdrawn from the patient. Other people claim that it is part of the natural dying process that patients increasingly lose interest in food or drink. Moreover, there is evidence that "terminal dehydration" may have a comforting effect on the dying patient by activating the body's endogenous analgesic mechanisms (Post, 2001). If artificial nutrition and hydration is continued, the dying process can be extended by several weeks. Decisions should be guided by the goal to minimise the patient's suffering and respect the patient's (actual or prior) choices. This requires a careful evaluation of the benefits and burdens of a continued artificial nutrition and hydration. A forced artificial nutrition or hydration seems to be inappropriate. Rather, assisted oral feeding should be encouraged.

Withdrawing versus withholding life-sustaining interventions

Many caregivers claim that there is an ethical difference between withholding and withdrawing life-sustaining interventions (Solomon et al., 1993). While it may be emotionally more difficult to stop a life-prolonging treatment than not to start it in the first place, there is no ethically relevant difference between withholding and withdrawing life-sustaining interventions (Beauchamp and Childress, 2001). Which treatment strategy is in the patient's best interests is all that matters from an ethical perspective. Especially if there is considerable uncertainty about the prospective benefit of an intervention, it might be better to start the treatment until a clearer assessment of the patient's prognosis and the net benefit of the intervention is possible. In contrast to withholding, starting a life-sustaining intervention is a reversible decision. Especially under great prognostic uncertainty, reversible decisions should be preferred to an irreversible decision. Therefore, the burden of proof seems to be greater in withholding than in withdrawing life-sustaining interventions.

Decisions about ending or extending life-sustaining treatment involve value judgments about the benefits, risk and burdens of interventions. The concept of futility should be used with great caution. Only in its strict sense, futility may justify physicians' unilateral decisions to withhold life-sustaining treatment. Generally, competent patients should decide autonomously whether life-supporting interventions should be continued. If patients lack full decision-making capacity, surrogates should nevertheless try to respect the patient's preferences and values whenever possible. Any trustworthy and clinically relevant advance directive should be followed. If no prior autonomous judgments exist, substituted judgments should be based on the patient's individual beliefs and values. If only little or nothing is known about the patient's preferences, surrogates must decide what they consider to be best for the patient. After withdrawal of a life-sustaining intervention, patients should receive compassionate and competent palliative care that allows them to die in dignity.

References

Beauchamp, T.L. and Childress, J.F., *Principles of biomedical ethics,* 5th edition, New York, Oxford University Press, 2001.

Buchanan, A.E. and Brock, D.W., *Deciding for others. The ethics of surrogate decision-making,* Cambridge University Press, 1990.

Emanuel, L.L., "Structured deliberation to improve decision-making for the seriously ill", *Hastings Center Report,* 25(6), 1995, pp. S14-18.

Kopelman, L.M., "Conceptual and moral disputes about futile and useful treatments", *Journal of Medical Philosophy,* 20(2), 1995, pp. 109-121.

Lo, B., *Resolving ethical dilemmas. A guide for clinicians,* Baltimore, Williams & Wilkins, 1995.

McCullough, L.B. and Ashton, C.M., "A methodology for teaching ethics in the clinical setting : a clinical handbook for medical ethics", *Theoretical Medicine,* 15, 1994, pp. 39-52.

Post, S.G., "Tube feeding and advanced progressive dementia", *Hastings Center Report,* 31(1), 2001, pp. 36-42.

Schneiderman, L.J., Jecker, N.S. and Jonson, A.R., "Medical futility : its meaning and ethical implications", *Annals of Internal Medicine,* 112, 1990, pp. 949-954.

Solomon, M.Z., O'Donnell, L., Jennings, B., Guilfoy, V., Wolf, S.M., Nolan, K. et al., "Decisions near the end of life : professional views on life-sustaining treatments", *American Journal of Public Health,* 83(1),1993, pp. 14-23.

Tomlinson, T. and Brody, H., "Futility and the ethics of resuscitation", *JAMA,* 264(10), 1990, pp. 1276-1280.

Truog, R.D., Brett, A.S. and Frader, J., "The problem with futility", *New England Journal of Medicine,* 1992, 326(23), 1560-4.

Youngner, S.J., "Who defines futility ?", *JAMA,* 260(14), 1988, pp. 2094-2095.

End-of-life reflections

by Bernard Kouchner

For almost a decade, as the French Minister for Health in Lionel Jospin's government, I sought to improve conditions for people in the closing stage of life. Pain, palliative care, euthanasia : a whole range of issues queued up to be addressed. These were the last matters I worked on as minister and I am sorry I failed to make more headway on what are vital questions. Reform in France has never been achieved overnight and I knew it would be hard to complete what I had undertaken. None the less, I reproach myself for having failed to do so.

More than regret, I feel real sadness. I lacked time, and perhaps I was not bold enough in my approach to a question of such fundamental importance. Euthanasia is a brutal word – one that I dislike for its very harshness on the ear – and every time it is used it evokes private memories or fears for the future. How will we end our lives? Will we suffer? Will we be capable of caring for and supporting those closest to us, of sparing them humiliation and pain? I have never met anyone who can discuss death without thinking of his or her own death and the deaths of loved ones.

I once knew a beautiful woman who was still young : without telling anyone of her decision, she ended her life using means available through an organisation that campaigns for "dignified" death.[1] The reaction of those closest to her was one of abandonment and betrayal. They have not yet overcome their immense grief and inability to comprehend. The woman had cancer and her treatment had been proceeding well. Although there were no signs of relapse, she probably felt that this was a possibility she should not have to face. She was free to take that view, just as those she left behind were free to suffer and go on suffering. Ever since, although I respect campaigners for euthanasia – I have held friendly discussions with them and, fundamentally, we take the same approach – I have been wary of proselytisers. That people should end their days in the way they wish, surrounded by those closest to them, is something I understand and approve of. But on occasions I have encountered a relent-

1.
Association pour le Droit de Mourir dans la Dignité (Association for the Right to Die with Dignity), or ADMD. See Catherine Leguay, *Mourir dans la dignité. Quand un médecin dit oui*, Robert Laffont, 2000.

less insistence on euthanasia which I find chilling. I am uncomfortable with the notion of death as a medical specialisation.

Ought I to have persuaded the government to rush through legislation on the end of life? I did not want to create a legal straitjacket, I was working towards a code of conduct, towards consensus and a standard practice that would be universally acceptable. To a certain extent we succeeded. I would have needed more time for discussion in order to avoid a clash between the advocates of palliative care – of whom I am one – and the advocates of euthanasia, in whose ranks I count myself in certain rare and specific circumstances.

We did a lot of work on the subject. We began in 2001 and 2002 at the Health Ministry with two days of courteous and respectful exchange between the supposedly opposing parties. It was not easy to engage in dialogue. We lacked a set of definitions and had to deal with conflicting prejudices.

The question of the end of life was raised. I was thinking in particular of deaths in intensive care, where five times out of ten the doctors disconnect the lifelines.[1] I believed that this decision could not be left to the goodwill or otherwise of the doctor. The law that made the practice a criminal offence had to be changed and that meant substituting teamwork for the arbitrary decision of a lone practitioner. Once a palliative care system had been established, at least in part, the way was clear for me to take the next step.

This type of debate was taking place all over Europe. Within our government there was little inter-ministerial discussion on the subject. At cabinet level we never openly debated social issues – it was not the appropriate forum. Once, however, at the Prime Minister's office, during an inter-ministerial meeting on draft legislation, the PM asked me whether reference to the ending of life should be slipped into the bill on the rights of the sick. Was it time to insist on introducing euthanasia? I sensed that he thought so but that he did not want to force my hand. I needed to organise several more meetings, more consultation at local level – in short, it seemed too soon.

I was wrong not to seize the opportunity, but the National Assembly was making heavy weather of the debate on

1.
Study carried out by
Dr Edouard Ferrand in
more than a hundred
intensive care units in
France.

bioethics and I felt that inserting a clause on the end of life into the bill on the rights of the sick would only add to the confusion. The resultant act already offers quite a lot : the right of both patients and doctors to refuse artificial prolongation of life ; a consent requirement for all forms of treatment ; and the right to die with dignity. I wanted to advance through persuasion on a subject where I am uncomfortable with the law as a blunt instrument. I am convinced that, had I had the few extra months I believed were available, I would have succeeded. The necessary majority would have come together. That said, divisions on the subject are highly sensitive. There are many on the left who are strongly opposed – and even more on the right. So yes, I have regrets. Had I taken a different line we would have had a law on the statute books. But what sort of law ? One that replaced death in hospital with a peaceful end at home ? One that eliminated suffering ? One that gave everyone freedom of choice ? As it is, we still lag several years behind Belgium, Spain and the Netherlands. François de Closets has fiercely censured my failure to act – my lack of "political courage".[1]

Opinion polls indicate that the French public was ready for change. People wanted reforms in the way that we deal with death. But how were we to respond ? I once spent a few weeks with some Dutch friends. The father of one of them had decided to die and had invited everyone to be there on a chosen day at a chosen hour. The period of waiting was hard – experiencing with the son and daughter-in-law just a fraction of their anguish, I wondered if this was really the best solution. A strange set of hoops to go through and a dreadful sense of pressure : would this type of arrangement be compatible with our own culture ? I think that, in order to facilitate death with freedom and dignity, the social and community environment needs to be improved. I find too much rigour and rigidity offensive. When I met the Dutch Health Minister, Ms Borst, she told me that she herself believed things were moving too fast and that doctors in the Netherlands had been somewhat overtaken by events. At the conferral of an honorary doctorate from Erasmus University, I had another opportunity of comparing the French and Dutch approaches. Ours is a culture

1.
De Closets, F., *La Dernière liberté*, Paris, Fayard, 2001.

steeped in Catholicism, which admits of connivance, secrecy, promises and dissembling. We need to curb these tendencies and strike a balance between the different factions and positions in the debate.

Had my own position been a hard and fast one, I would have made it known. Over the two days of discussions at the ministry with doctors, various organisations, journalists and philosophers, I was alive to the arguments on all sides, and particularly to a fresh and less ideological approach to palliative care, a softening, rather than a blurring, of positions. I was also aware of the mental blocks that exist.

I am familiar with the world of palliative care. I have made a number of visits to the Gardanne hospice, and I count the people there as friends. I have supported them in many different situations. I have also learned a lot from them, as I have from the Jeanne Garnier House in Paris, from the Association François-Xavier Bagnoud, and from the palliative care organisation Jusqu'à la Mort Accompagner la Vie (JALMALV), with Françoise Glorion and her friends. I did my utmost to get funding for expansion at Gardanne and I am proud to have been successful. At the same time I have been taken aback by this specialisation in death. What I would like to see – and this is why my own position is not cut and dried – is all doctors, with their mission to serve life, becoming doctors of both life and death, so that death would be part of their lives. One result of the meetings, at which we made a great deal of progress, was to take the concept of assisted suicide out of the picture. That in itself helped to clarify matters. On the remaining aspects of the question, however, we still have some way to go.

This is highly sensitive territory and we have to weigh our words with care. The film *C'est la vie* – with Jacques Dutronc and Sandrine Bonnaire – which tackles the subject is tremendously powerful. But it was not a hit with the French public, and nor, really, was Antoine Audouard's book[1] despite some opinion polls that have been quoted. Why should this be so? The campaigners for palliative care who work at Gardanne, in an environment where great gentleness and great determination go hand in hand, never speak of euthanasia. At the mere

1.
Audouard, A., *Une maison au bord du monde*, Paris, Gallimard, 2001.

mention of the word they fall silent and one can sense emotional walls going up. It is as if the doctors of the dying had to defend themselves against what Marguerite Duras called "the malady of death". As if the act of helping dying people to part from their loved ones was somehow shameful.

My own concern with the subject goes back a long way. My real discovery of palliative care was in connection with the death of François Mitterrand – a major political figure who taught me a lot about life (not all of it pleasant) and whom I often miss. He told me about the palliative care unit at the Cité Universitaire hospital and I visited it. I was struck by the obvious support the patients were being given. I learned from the experience and teaching of my friend Doctor Jean-Pierre Tarot, who was with François Mitterrand right to the end. I invited him to my office and it was he who inspired my reforms. I also met Marie de Hennezel. I have read her books[1] and am familiar with her campaign, even if I do not always agree with her rejection of elective, dignified death and take issue with a dimension of her work that I regard as "theological". I trust she will forgive me summarising it like that.

I believe that in more than 90% of cases the end of life can be transformed, with pain and suffering eliminated through the palliative care that my colleagues and I have developed over a period of years. Yet there is a residual mental block. This has to be faced. As soon as I mention elective death, some of my friends who work in palliative care simply pull down the shutters.

We have come a long way. For many years, death was a forbidden subject. Those who broached it were criticised. The resistance was mainly rooted in medical certainties. Apparently there could be no exception to the doctor's ethical and social imperative not to bring about death. It was difficult, in routine practice, to address the subject. Thanks to volunteers like Françoise Glorion and the team at Gardanne, the situation has moved on. The issues of palliative care, gentle death and euthanasia take us to what constitutes the final frontier for an affluent society that lacks certainties and is reluctant to engage in debate. In France, such matters used not to be spoken of – by doctors or anyone else – or else they were alluded to fleet-

1.
De Hennezel, M., *La Mort intime*, with a preface by François Mitterrand, Paris, Robert Laffont, 1995.

ingly in secretive tones. Students at medical school were taught nothing about these questions. It was the patients (an ambiguous word with an implication of suffering) who, just a few years ago, threw off the shackles and got debate going. And, as in all great campaigns, the debate took place at personal cost to some individuals. Is it really a betrayal, a sin, a breach of religious faith, to help an aware human being to die?

Opponents used to ask me about my own practice as a doctor in the field of humanitarian aid. At one point these exchanges took a somewhat polemical turn because I said that I had helped people to die in various wars. I said this because it was true. Those people who were outraged have no concept of death and pain in wartime. They do not know what it means. I believe their reaction stemmed from the fact that death – or at least death here in France, which for 70% of us takes place in hospital – is still a taboo subject. It is not so for me.

I have had to hasten the end for both soldiers and civilians who have pleaded with me to do so. There was a fifteen-year-old Palestinian fighter, for example, who took the full force of a rocket fired from the Christian suburb of Achrafieh. He had multiple injuries : his abdomen, spleen and liver were a pulp. He was losing so much blood that transfusion or surgery would have been no use ; none the less we were, of course, getting ready to attempt the impossible in our makeshift hospital in a cellar in Borg Hamoud-Nabaa. The young man was still conscious and knew he was going to die. As I had learned in Biafra, people wounded in war often sense this. He was screaming, he could not take any more and he wanted it to be over. We had no blood. For days and nights on end, a battle had been raging. We had only a little precious morphine left. I consulted the members of the team, as was our frequent practice. Despite their differences of training, religion and nationality, none raised any objection. I could tell of similar cases during the fall of Saigon, in Biafra, in the Middle East, southern Sudan or Liberia. This type of unhappy outcome, the desperation for an end to pain, in situations where the gap between needs and resources is unimaginable by our own standards, bears no relation to the debate about ending life in France. Such memories bring me no satisfaction, no delusions of power. When I recall all those unfortunates I still grieve.

The situation in France is quite different. Like all doctors, I have encountered people with dreadful afflictions, who have spent long years suffering and have fought right to the end. Others could have lived longer but did not want to. None of us really knows how we will react to the news that death is imminent. I remember a patient who came to me in Cochin hospital for a digestive-tract endoscopy: a comfortably-off factory owner and former member of the Resistance. I suspected he had a gastric tumour. He had made me swear to tell him truthfully the results of his test. He had explained about his responsibilities to his workforce, his family and his children, while shaking my hand so hard that he twisted my arm. I still remember the hug he gave me. He said, too, that we understood one another, that he had fought in the war and had looked death in the face. When he came back I gave him his results, choosing my words with some care, for he did have cancer. He seized my arm again and said forcefully: "Look me in the eye when you speak to me: you promised you would tell me the truth!" I was most uncomfortable, for doctors in France are taught to shield the patient. I looked him in the eye and said: "If I were you, with abnormal histology like this I'd arrange for surgery immediately." "Thank you, doctor," he replied, "that can't have been easy for you." He embraced me and then left with the young woman who was waiting for him outside. The next day, without a word to his family or his workforce, he committed suicide.

So what is my own position? It is clear to me that everyone would wish to be able to die at home, surrounded by family, at peace and able to crack a last joke or raise a grin. Does that mean "pressing a little harder on the syringe"? It is a question that will have to be answered sooner or later because it has to do with the other person's freedom as well as dignity. I am in full agreement with the sociologist Philippe Bataille, who said during our discussions at the ministry: "This is a question for society as a whole."

Some three out of four French people die in hospital, half of them in intensive care, frequently after the decision has had to be taken to withdraw treatment, switch off the machines or indeed press a little harder on the morphine syringe to make the end easier. Medicine has progressed to such an extent that it is developing the capacity to keep almost anyone alive virtually indefinitely. The figures will get worse unless we do something. In the United States, 90% of people die in hospital, almost 80% of them following a decision by doctors. Is this what we want? If it is, then the doctors need to be told, loudly and clearly, so they can stop worrying that they will be hauled before the courts for manslaughter. We have to stop behaving as if euthanasia did not exist. It is not as easy as it used to be to identify precisely the point at which artificially prolonging life begins. Every day, medical technology is making the divide between life and death less clear cut. The medical world and we, as a society, need to accept the resultant transformation in the circumstances of death.

Not all doctors are in agreement. I realise that death is not a medical procedure : that would be too easy. Death is a part of life and life is not solely in the gift of doctors. Patients are asking doctors to join with them in dealing with an aspect of their pathology. Doctors are free to refuse, as they did for many years in relation to pain and Aids. But times have changed. We should not be too quick to forget the arguments and efforts that were needed to change medical practitioners' attitudes to pain and palliative care. Every victory in this has been a defeat for received ideas, which are so deep-seated in medicine.

We also have to recognise that certain patients can be every bit as conservative as certain doctors. There are people who believe that pain is not a medical problem, but a part of life. It is a familiar refrain : redemption achieved through pain ; suffering as the measure of courage and humanity. The tradition is deeply rooted in our civilisation, and this I also understand. You cannot force people. The right to interfere ceases if the victim does not want assistance. But in the health field, a right of interference still needs introducing.

What is required is openness and interpersonal honesty, for this is an issue that is deeply political, in the best sense of the word – and the measure of true politics is its ability to tackle precisely this type of problem.

In social debates of this kind, where religious and philosophical views collide, the role of a minister is to move things on : to put himself in the shoes of the various parties. While it is true that death is part of life, it cannot be entirely de-medicalised. The patient must have as much say as the doctor : it is a question of freedom. Some people take the view, from religious conviction, that the day and hour of their death are not theirs to choose. Others take an opposite view : that there is little enough they can control, and that electing the time of their death, if they can do so, is their last act of freedom. Surely it is possible to respect individuals' differing conceptions of human freedom? The individual, and only the individual, can decide whether they prefer to leave the hour of their death in the hands of fate, the hands of God or the hands of the doctor. The individual, and only the individual, can delimit or define their own freedom. At the same time, the task of the practitioner is to be of service, to ease suffering and to offer care and support. The former head of the French Medical Council, Bernard Glorion, put it very well when he said : "Let there be no more talk of euthanasia; let us talk, rather, of supporting the dying." I agree with him. Let us tackle the problem of supporting the dying right to the end. My function as minister was to set change in motion and to guide a process towards an agreed position if possible. But no consensus emerged. This means that the task of the minister now is to take a decision. It is not – happily – to impose their own beliefs, whatever they might be.

We managed to reach agreement on use of the term "ending treatment" and that was a step forward. In the sensitive territory that has been termed "passive euthanasia", doctors who "gently" disconnected lifelines could find themselves accused of a criminal offence. Together, working with doctors and patients' associations, we made some progress. My hope was to bring about a change of attitudes in our society, to introduce greater gentleness but also a greater sense of involvement. If politics is about anything, surely it is about curbing and channelling forms of violence? I am both a politician and a doctor. I am glad that I know something about forms of human violence, and death – like war – is one of the most mysterious areas in which violence is present. I have spent time with both death and war, and I felt that I was in the right place.

If we look beyond the French experience, we see that in the United States, for example, the decision is taken, first and foremost, by the patient. In France, on the other hand, we hear doctors defending their own role, sometimes quite courageously, asserting that they must have the final say. It is an old French tradition that the doctor knows best – and it has been an honourable tradition. While I have done my best to respect this medical sovereignty, it no longer reflects the way society has developed. If we are not careful, a major schism is going to develop between our more and more demanding society and a medical corps that is stretched to its limits. General practice is not the same job that it was twenty years ago. Confidence needs to be restored. The Hippocratic tradition has been diverted from its original purpose and we have to get to grips with that. The doctor is no longer in sole command. Patients today are infinitely better informed than they were in the past, and a number of doctors are going to find themselves in very uncomfortable situations. Specialising in death is not easy, so let us not leave those who do so isolated.

In the Latin countries the importance of doctors was once enshrined in the system. The medieval physician's slogan was, "I treated him. God cured him." The medical profession ranked next to the clergy. Today such status is impossible. There is a residue of sacredness but it is disappearing under the influence of Protestantism. It is no accident that the latest legislation takes its inspiration from the Netherlands, or that certain American states, such as Oregon, led the way in this regard. Ten years ago Oregon introduced a systematic procedure whereby patients are invited to discuss with the doctor precisely what they want to happen if death draws near, and – again with the doctor – to set their wishes down on paper. Some forty per cent of patients elect to return home in order to die with their families around them. I hope that our own legislation on palliative care has paved the way for this return to the home.

I would hope that people will again go home to die despite the mechanisation of our society. I have seen too many people dying in hospital, often in inhuman conditions. Whatever the cost, we must try to improve the environment for death in hospital. The very buildings and rooms are unsuitable. Supporting a member of the family in his or her last hours in hospital is an ordeal on both sides. What have people done to deserve that? When we go to see a family member or friend who is dying, or has died, in hospital, we face all sorts of problems. Where do we wait? Our very presence is an embarrassment to others and a trial for ourselves. Where will the body be taken? Does not the unit shut at six o'clock? Will the relatives who have to work late still be able to see the body this evening? The lack of respect is shocking. We will be told yet again that more staff are needed, and demonstrations will be held – and it is true that more staff are needed. But the situation has to be improved. We cannot go on treating every death in hospital as a nasty surprise.

We have undergone a peculiar change inasmuch as we have cut families off from death. We have cut ourselves off from death – artificially – and at the same time we flounder around in a society that takes precautions to ridiculous extremes. Legions of officials are employed to keep the quality of our beefburgers under permanent surveillance but we are told nothing at all about death. What sense does such a society make? It is completely turned on its head. I find all this outrageous. It is time for a complete change – a revolution. And why not? Nothing short of taking bulldozers to our towns and cities will enable old people to live close to young people – not necessarily with the young, but close to them. We have the money to put things right. We need to tear down our present way of life in order to build some dignity.

One day it will then be up to you to decide. They say that happiness is not a matter for policy, but unhappiness is. That being so, we need policies that will allow us to choose how we die. Once the policies are in place, let each of us make his or her own choice.

Euthanasia and the right to life[1] – The Pretty case

by Christian Byk

How, conceptually, does the right to life (legal protection of one of humanity's fundamental values) connect with euthanasia (concern for a "good" death)?

The paradox is all the greater in that its legal implication seems to be that the effect of applying a recognised human right, the right to life, could be a desired death; unless the pro-euthanasia case is simply viewed as a social phenomenon with the force of the right to life ranged against it.

Some see the right to life as a safeguard against euthanasia, others as its Trojan horse. Considered in those terms, the euthanasia issue certainly poses questions about control of life and what meaning life has for us.

The medicalisation of death (Ariès, 1977; Morin, 1976) is a clear manifestation of this (new) way of seeing things: it shifts the place of death (into hospital), changes the people involved (or, at least, the family is no longer in the foreground), and splits the timeframe into stages, with increasing involvement of medical technology at each successive stage.

The fact is that the picture of death which this presents is one we find unbearable and inhuman, not so much because it breaks with time-honoured rites and customs our new ways of life have led us to abandon, but because medicine seems here to be breaking its promises. Having given us control of procreation and lengthened our lives, how can it now refuse us choice of our time of death?

As death approaches, are we to lose the personal autonomy which has been steadily extended as medicine and science have advanced and the conquest of which as a right is the symbol of our human rights society (Prieur, 1999)?

And yet human rights law seems loftily to ignore exercise of individual autonomy with respect to death.

1.
I dedicate this paper to my friend, Ferdinando Albanese, a pioneer of bioethics in the Council of Europe, who died in November 2001 in the same circumstances as Mrs Pretty.

Until the Pretty decision (apart from a negative opinion given by the CDBI in the late 1980s in response to an application by the Dutch Government), the European Convention on Human Rights had not come up against the euthanasia issue. It is true that as early as 1976 the Parliamentary Assembly of the Council of Europe pronounced against prolonging life by technological means (Resolution 613 (1976) on the rights of the sick and dying, and Recommendation 779 (1976)) and Article 9 of the Convention on Human Rights and Biomedicine requires that account be taken of previously expressed wishes, including refusal of consent (though they are not binding), but it was only in the context preceding the Pretty judgment, with Recommendation 1418 (1999) (on protection of the human rights and dignity of the terminally ill and dying), that an explicitly restrictive position was stated, maintaining the absolute prohibition on intentionally ending the lives of the dying and terminally ill ("[their] wish to die never constitutes any legal claim to die at the hand of another person"). After this recommendation, the CDBI was instructed by the Committee of Ministers to draft a report on national legislation and practices. States' replies to the questionnaire on euthanasia were published on 20 January 2003.

True, this silence is as eloquent, in terms of human freedom, as criminal law's disengagement from matters of suicide. But there is more to this silence than affirmation of a freedom : it is also a refusal to discuss controlled death as part of life. When it was called upon to deliver judgment in the Pretty case, the European Court of Human Rights held that the right to life did not include the right to die (I), but conceded that the question of euthanasia involved exercise of personal autonomy (II), in our view opening the way to some degree of recognition of assisted suicide.

I. The right to life does not legitimise euthanasia

It probably took a humanly exceptional case to force the law out of its silence. Diane Pretty, who was paralysed by a neuro-degenerative disease that would in a short time result in death through respiratory failure, was such a case. She was in full command of her mental faculties and wanted her husband's assistance in putting an end to her life in order to avoid the distress and suffering of the final stages of her illness.

She maintained that the British authorities' refusal to guarantee that her husband would not be prosecuted for this contravened her right to life. Put in this way, the question could no longer be settled simply by looking at her case compassionately.

The Court had to decide whether the right to life, like the right to procreate in domestic law, had two aspects, one positive (prohibiting any interference with life), the other negative (helping someone to end a life without dignity)?

The Court decided that Article 2 did not include a right to self-determination. Nor could Article 3 be invoked to force the state to comply with the applicant's request.

A. ECHR Article 2 does not establish a right to self-determination

The applicant put forward a number of arguments in support of a right to die.

The refusal of the Director of Public Prosecutions (DPP) to give an undertaking that her husband would not be prosecuted for assisting her in her wish to end her life was, she contended, a direct infringement of her right to die as implicit in Article 2 of the Convention, otherwise those countries in which assisted suicide was not unlawful would be in breach of the Convention.

Contravention of the right to die

Does a state's refusal to lend the public authorities' assistance to, or allow someone else to assist, a person who wants to die constitute a breach of ECHR Article 2 ("Everyone's right to life shall be protected by law")?

This was what the applicant claimed when she argued that, since Article 2 protected not only life but the right to life, it implicitly recognised the individual's right to self-determination in matters of life and death.

Repeating and endorsing the arguments put forward by the British courts[1] in dismissing Mrs Pretty's domestic appeal, the Court, while stating that Article 2 of the Convention could result in the state's having positive duties, kept to a classic, uncomplicated interpretation of Article 2.

Article 2 as creating positive obligations

First, the Court sought to deliver a message, namely that it did not confine itself to a literal reading of Article 2 and did not interpret it strictly. It noted: "The text of Article 2 expressly regulates the deliberate or intended use of lethal force by state agents. It has been interpreted, however, as covering not only intentional killing but also the situations where it is permitted to 'use force' which may result, as an unintended outcome, in the deprivation of life."[2]

It also pointed out that the state's duties were not confined to refraining from intentional and unlawful taking of life.

Appropriate steps had to be taken to put in place "law enforcement machinery for the prevention, suppression and sanctioning of breaches [of criminal law provisions]". In certain circumstances the authorities even had a positive obligation to take preventive operational measures to protect an individual whose life was at risk.

The domestic courts had referred here to the case of Osman v. the United Kingdom,[3] in which the applicants had accused the United Kingdom of failing to protect the right to life of the second applicant and his deceased father. The Court itself cited the case of Keenan v. the United Kingdom,[4] in which Article 2 had been found to apply to the situation of a young mentally ill prisoner who had committed suicide in prison.

But while there was a positive obligation which was all the more binding where someone was in police custody or prison and therefore under the state's control, all the cases cited had been concerned with measures to prevent death. Positive measures to enable someone to die would only be acceptable if Article 2 were interpreted as also involving a negative aspect, and this the Court refused to do.

1.
House of Lords, ruling of 29 November 2001, The Queen on the Application of Mrs Diane Pretty v. the Director of Public Prosecutions and Secretary of State for the Home Department.

2.
Pretty v. the United Kingdom (Section IV), Application No. 2346/02, judgment of 29 April 2002, paragraph 38.

3.
Osman v. the United Kingdom, 28 October 1998, *Reports* 1998-VIII, paragraph 115.

4.
Keenan v. the United Kingdom (Section III), Application No. 27229/95, ECHR 2001-III, paragraph 91.

Does Article 2 confer a right not to act ?

If Article 2 established a right to self-determination with respect to life and death and if someone was so disabled that they were unable to do anything to bring about their own death, it necessarily followed, Mrs Pretty argued, that they had a right to be killed by a third party and that the state would be in breach of the Convention if it interfered in the exercise of that right.[1]

While observing, like the House of Lords, that some of the rights guaranteed by the Convention had been interpreted as establishing rights to act, the Court considered that Article 2 took a quite different approach.

There are articles that confer diametrically opposite rights : Article 9 confers a right not to be compelled to express one's thoughts or divulge one's convictions, Article 11 confers not only a right to join an association but also a right not to, and Article 12 can be interpreted as also conferring a right not to marry.

But those articles are concerned with freedoms and, as the Court noted, "a freedom implies some measure of choice as to its exercise".[2] However, not all the articles of the Convention follow that model. The House of Lords observed : "It cannot, however, be suggested [...] that Articles 3 [prohibition of torture], 4 [slavery], 5 [arbitrary detention] and 6 [fair trial] confer an implied right to do or experience the opposite of that which the articles guarantee."[3]

The existence of a right to die in the light of changes in member states' positive law

In the absence of legal arguments intrinsic to the wording of Article 2, could Mrs Pretty rely upon extrinsic considerations – here, changes in positive law in member states – to persuade the Court to interpret Article 2 more broadly ?

We know that the Netherlands, followed by Belgium, have "legalised" assisted suicide, that Swiss criminal law takes altruistic or egotistical motives into account, and that pressure of public opinion in many countries in favour of facilitating a dignified death for terminally ill patients has given rise to

1.
Pretty v. the United Kingdom, op. cit., paragraph 35.

2.
Ibid., paragraph 39.

3.
See note 1, p.112.

considerable social debate which has included discussion about amending the law to make it more favourable to assisted suicide[1].

Mrs Pretty therefore had reason to hope that the Court might view these developments as significant if Article 2 were to be interpreted with full regard to shifts in law and thinking in the member states. That is implicit in her asking, doubtless somewhat provocatively, whether, if the Convention did not recognise a right to die, the countries which allowed assisted suicide were not in breach of it.

Obviously the turn in European debate has not convinced the Court that, in the context of a right as fundamental as the right to life, interpretation needs to change in the light of changing attitudes.

The Court, indeed, was explicit, radical even, on this point: Article 2, it said, "is unconcerned with issues to do with the quality of living or what a person chooses to do with his or her life," and it concluded that "Article 2 cannot, without a distortion of language, be interpreted as conferring the diametrically opposed right, namely a right to die."[2]

It held that "the extent to which a state permits, or seeks to regulate, the possibility for the infliction of harm on individuals at liberty, by their own or another's hand, may raise conflicting considerations of personal freedom and the public interest,"[3] but the situation was very different in the present case where the proposition was that the United Kingdom had failed in its obligations under Article 2 of the Convention. In other words, even had the applicant proved that the situation in states that allow assisted suicide is not contrary to Article 2, that in itself would still not have shown the United Kingdom to be in breach of its obligations on account of not allowing assisted suicide. Even if the legislation in countries which allow assisted suicide does not infringe the Convention, that does not mean the legislation of those that do not allow it is in breach of Article 2.

As the Court went on to show in regard to the alleged infringement of Article 3, no provision of the Convention can require a state "to sanction actions intended to terminate life".

1.
Byk, C., "La revendication individuelle face à la mort: approche comparatiste des questions posées par l'interruption de traitement, l'euthanasie et l'aide au suicide", *Revue Générale de Droit*, University of Ottawa, 1998, p. 209, and CDBI, replies to the questionnaire on euthanasia, Council of Europe, Strasbourg, 20 January 2003.

2.
Pretty v. the United Kingdom, op. cit., paragraph 39.

3.
Ibid., paragraph 41.

B. No Article 3 obligation on states to act against life

Mrs Pretty maintained that the blanket ban on assisted suicide in English law was contrary to the absolute right in Article 3 not to be subjected to inhuman or degrading treatment.

The Court rejected that argument, refusing to regard the situation in which the applicant found herself as "treatment" for the purposes of Article 3, which had to be interpreted in harmony with Article 2.

No "treatment" within the meaning of Article 3

According to the applicant, the disputed decision of the British authorities which denied her the right to her husband's help in terminating her life meant that her illness would run its course and she would therefore have to endure suffering and indignity.[1]

The Court pointed out that in the light of the case-law, Article 3 "may be described in general terms as imposing a primarily negative obligation on states to refrain from inflicting serious harm on persons within their jurisdiction".[2]

However, in view of the importance of Article 3, a degree of flexibility had been adopted in applying it. In particular, it had been held that, for the purposes of Article 3 combined with Article 1, which required Contracting Parties to secure to everyone within their jurisdiction the rights and freedoms defined in the Convention, states were under an obligation to take positive measures against inhuman and degrading treatment, including such treatment of vulnerable persons by private individuals.[3] But it was still necessary for the facts at issue to fall within the scope of "treatment" within the meaning of Article 3.

The respondent government had not itself inflicted any ill-treatment on the applicant and she was not complaining that she had not received adequate care from the state medical authorities. The Court noted: "The situation of the applicant is therefore not comparable with the case of D. v. the United Kingdom, in which an Aids sufferer was threatened with removal from the United Kingdom to the island of St Kitts, where no effective medical [...] treatment for his illness was

1.
Ibid., paragraph 44.

2.
Ibid., paragraph 50.

3.
Judgment in A. v. the United Kingdom, 23 September 1998, *Reports* 1998-VI, p. 2699, and in Z. and Others v. the United Kingdom (GC), 20392/95, ECHR 2001-V.

available and he would have been exposed to the risk of dying under the most distressing circumstances."[1]

As we have seen, the issues here were the DPP's refusal to undertake not to prosecute the applicant's husband and the British prohibition on assisted suicide, creating a situation which, Mrs Pretty said, constituted inhuman and degrading treatment for which the state was responsible in so far as it did not allow her to protect herself from the suffering she would endure in the final stages of her illness.[2]

The Court regarded that claim as placing "a new and extended construction on the concept of treatment, which [...] goes beyond the ordinary meaning of the word."

Here it concurred with the House of Lords, which had found: "By no legitimate process of interpretation can that refusal be held to fall within the negative prohibition of Article 3." With regard to states' possibly having a positive obligation, the Court noted that "the positive obligation on the part of the state which is invoked in the present case would not involve the removal or mitigation of harm". The brevity of the Court's reasons and its reluctance to open up the interpretation of Article 3 may be surprising, but should be seen as reflecting a desire for consistency in the interpretation of Article 2.

An interpretation of Article 3 consistent with Article 2

The Court began its observations on the complaint of violation of Article 3 by saying: "Article 3 of the Convention, together with Article 2, must be regarded as one of the most fundamental provisions of the Convention and as enshrining core values of the democratic societies making up the Council of Europe."[3] It followed that, while the Court must take a dynamic and flexible approach to the interpretation of the Convention, which was a living instrument, any interpretation must also accord with the fundamental objectives of the Convention and its coherence as a system of human rights protection.[4]

Consequently "Article 3 must be construed in harmony with Article 2, which has hitherto been associated with it as reflecting basic values respected by democratic societies." The Court continued: "Article 2 of the Convention is first and foremost a

1.
Pretty v the United Kingdom, op. cit., paragraph 53.

2.
Ibid., paragraph 54.

3.
Ibid., paragraph 49.

4.
Ibid., paragraph 54.

prohibition on the use of lethal force or other conduct which might lead to the death of a human being and does not confer any claim on an individual to require a state to permit or facilitate his or her death."[1]

For that reason "the positive obligation on the part of the state which is invoked [...] would require that the state sanction actions intended to terminate life, an obligation that cannot be derived from Article 3 of the Convention".[2]

The Court none the less expressed sympathy with the applicant and, as often in judge-made law, took the opportunity to establish an advance in case-law though rejecting the appeal: for the first time Article 8 of the ECHR was here construed as the legal expression of the principle of personal autonomy and, in the deliberations on assisted suicide, the concept of quality of life was taken into account.

II. Recognition of personal autonomy and of the concept of quality of life

It is because the right to life solely expresses the primacy we accord life as the essential value, without which human beings cannot enjoy any of the freedoms and rights afforded them, that the right to life consists solely in a right to preserve and protect human life. Hence its special status, both substantive and procedural, in the ECHR: like Article 3, it is an absolute right.

And yet, compassion and sympathy apart, can the law ignore the increasing suffering of those whose plight is identical to Mrs Pretty's and the resulting loss of human dignity (not that it should accede to all expressed wishes, but expression of wishes does reflect exercise of our freedoms, which are guaranteed by the European Convention on Human Rights)?

Provided that exercise of freedoms does not upset the balance between the individual's interests and society's interests as defined by the Convention, the desire for death deserves consideration because allowing individuals to make their own life choices is not only central to the philosophy of human rights but also a guarantee of democracy.

1.
Ibid., paragraph 54.

2.
Ibid., paragraph 55.

Article 8 of the Convention is obviously the locus of this debate, not only because the concept of "private life" is very broad, but also because, as can be seen from its application to the facts of this case, it raises questions of discrimination and inequality with respect to persons who, like the applicant, freely and repeatedly express a clearly stated wish at the same time as being completely unable, because of their physical condition, to accomplish that wish, even when the balance is struck between their personal interests and the interests of the community.

The Court opened the way to making Article 8 applicable to distressing end-of-life situations by having the perspicacity to recognise, for the first time, that "the notion of personal autonomy is an important principle underlying the interpretation of [...] [the] guarantees [of Article 8]". As for giving effect to the principle, it applied it tentatively (and will doubtless reinforce it in future), refusing to acknowledge, for reasons of (criminal) policy and because the state interference was not disproportionate, the discrimination which applying the contested law created with regard to exercise of the right to autonomy of people with physical disabilities.

A. The principle of personal autonomy underlies interpretation of the Article 8 guarantees

Quite apart from the rejection of Mrs Pretty's case, which understandably captured the attention of readers of the judgment as a result both of the human dilemma and the media coverage, in our opinion the real import of the decision lies in the statement that Article 8 of the Convention is the legal expression of the principle of personal autonomy.

Pragmatism

What should arouse the wrath of more than a few commentators – especially those from continental systems – in the freedom the Court has taken with the balances in the Convention (Kayser, 1990) is rather, as we see it, the evidence of a gradual shift over the years – a constant drift in the view of the Court's detractors – in the shape of pragmatic interpretation of the concept of "private life".

From the case-law of the Convention, the view emerges that the concept of private life "is a broad term not susceptible to exhaustive definition".

As the Court has pointed out, it "covers the physical and psychological integrity of a person", and can sometimes embrace aspects of an individual's physical and social identity.

Gender identification, name and sexual orientation and sexual life are some of the things that fall within the personal sphere protected by Article 8. It also protects "a right to personal development, and the right to establish and develop relationships with other human beings and the outside world".[1]

It is the potential range of situations connected with the life choices an individual may make and the effects both on their physical and psychological integrity and on the organisation of society that has led the Court to connect Article 8 and exercise of individual freedom in the sense of the right to self-determination.

In the Pretty judgment, to avoid being accused of inventing a new right on the basis of a text that in no way contained it (as happened to the United States Supreme Court in the famous case of Roe v. Wade[2] in connection with the right of privacy), the Court took care to state that no previous case had established any right to self-determination as such in Article 8 of the Convention.[3]

Nevertheless, on the basis of the case-law, and while it was not in itself a right, the Court held that "the notion of personal autonomy was an important principle underlying the interpretation of the Article 8 guarantees".[4]

The "demand" for a right to die with assistance therefore has to be examined in the light of that principle.

"The concept of quality of life" and its meaning under Article 8 of the ECHR

Having laid down the principle that Article 8 of the ECHR should be construed in the light of the concept of personal autonomy, the Court was bound to reject the British Government's argument that the right to private life could not encapsulate a right to die with assistance, just as the identical

1.
Ibid., paragraph 61.

2.
Roe v. Wade 410 US 113 (1973).

3.
Pretty v. the United Kingdom, op. cit., paragraph 61.

4.
Ibid., paragraph 61.

position taken by the authorities in relation to abortion had once been rejected by the European Commission of Human Rights.

"The Court would observe that the ability to conduct one's life in a manner of one's own choosing may also include the opportunity to pursue activities perceived to be of a physically or morally harmful or dangerous nature for the individual concerned." The Court went on to say that "even where the conduct poses a danger to health or, arguably, where it is of a life-threatening nature, the case-law of the Convention institutions has regarded the state's imposition of compulsory or criminal measures as impinging on the private life of the applicant within the scope of Article 8, paragraph 1".[1]

The Court here delivered itself of something of an obiter dictum about medical treatment. Carrying on from its comments on the case-law, it expressed the view that "the imposition of medical treatment, without the consent of a mentally competent adult patient, would interfere with a person's physical integrity in a manner capable of engaging the rights protected under Article 8, paragraph 1, of the Convention".[2]

But, above all, it fully recognised that the situation at issue was different for purposes of the applicability of Article 8, paragraph 1.

"The applicant is suffering from the devastating effects of a degenerative disease which will cause her condition to deteriorate further and increase her physical and mental suffering. She wishes to mitigate that suffering by exercising a choice to end her life with the assistance of her husband."

Courageously and in measured language, the Court went on to state that "the way she chooses to pass the closing moments of her life is part of the act of living, and she has a right to ask that this too must be respected".[3]

With the same restraint and clear-sightedness, it then gave its reasoning : "The very essence of the Convention is respect for human dignity and human freedom. Without in any way negating the principle of sanctity of life protected under the

1.
Ibid., paragraph 62.

2.
Ibid., paragraph 63.

3.
Ibid., paragraph 64.

Convention, the Court considers that it is under Article 8 that notions of the quality of life take on significance."[1]

The use of the expression "quality of life" may certainly be regretted but, lest it be taken as opening the way to every kind of abuse, the Court explained to what situation it applied: "In an era of growing medical sophistication combined with longer life expectancies, many people are concerned that they should not be forced to linger on in old age or in states of advanced physical or mental decrepitude which conflict with strongly held ideas of self and personal identity."[2]

It concluded: "The applicant in this case is prevented by law from exercising her choice to avoid what she considers will be an undignified and distressing end to her life. The Court is not prepared to exclude that this constitutes an interference with her right to respect for private life as guaranteed under Article 8, paragraph 1, of the Convention."[3]

It only remained to examine whether or not that interference was compatible with the second paragraph of Article 8 and with Article 14, as relied upon by the applicant, when taken together with Article 8. Here the Court, doubtless concerned about the effects of this first decision, gave the needs of criminal policy precedence over the circumstances of individuals whom illness completely prevented from putting their wishes into effect without assistance.

B. Avoiding the judgment's being interpreted as a general precedent

Granted that the prohibition on assisted suicide constituted interference with the protection of private life, the only question was whether the interference was warranted. Did it correspond to a pressing social need and, in particular, was it proportionate to the legitimate aim pursued?[4]

Having considered the question of proportionateness, the Court in fact found the interference to be reconcilable both with Article 8, paragraph 2, of the ECHR and with Article 14 (the principle of non-discrimination) taken together with Article 8.

1.
Ibid., paragraph 65.

2.
Ibid., paragraph 65.
3.
Ibid., paragraph 67.

4.
Ibid., paragraph 70.

Reconciling the interference with Article 8, paragraph 2: a conciliatory Court

Having stated that "in determining whether an interference is 'necessary in a democratic society', the Court will take into account that a margin of appreciation is left to the national authorities" and that "the margin of appreciation has been found to be narrow as regards interferences in the intimate area of an individual's sexual life", the Court decided that the subject of the present case could not "be regarded as of the same nature, or as attracting the same reasoning".[1]

Taking care to refute the argument of the British Government, which had justified its decision by arguing "that the applicant, as a person who is both contemplating suicide and severely disabled, must be regarded as vulnerable",[2] the Court focused on the applicant's argument "attack[ing] in particular the blanket nature of the ban on assisted suicide as failing to take into account her situation as a mentally competent adult who knows her own mind, who is free from pressure and who has made a fully informed and voluntary decision, and therefore cannot be regarded as vulnerable and requiring protection".[3]

It flatly rejected it, finding, in agreement with the House of Lords and the Canadian Supreme Court,[4] that "states are entitled to regulate through the operation of the general criminal law activities which are detrimental to the life and safety of other individuals" and that "[the] more serious the harm involved the more heavily will weigh in the balance considerations of public health and safety against the countervailing principle of personal autonomy".[5]

Up to this point the reasoning is admirably rigorous but when the Court applies it to the legislation at issue it incurs, in our view, two criticisms.

In the first place, there seems to be an inconsistency.

Having just made the point that the applicant could not be classed as vulnerable, it justified its strict line on margin of appreciation on the sole ground of protecting the vulnerable.

It stated : "The law in issue in this case [...] was designed to safeguard life by protecting the weak and vulnerable and espe-

1.
Ibid., paragraph 71.

2.
Ibid., paragraph 73.

3.
Ibid., paragraph 72.

4.
Supreme Court of Canada, Rodriguez v. British Columbia (1993), 3RCS, 519.

5.
Pretty v. the United Kingdom, op. cit., paragraph 74.

cially those who are not in a condition to take informed decisions," but aware of the discrepancy between this statement and Mrs Pretty's determination, which it had seen for itself, it added, as if in embarrassment : "Doubtless the condition of terminally ill individuals will vary. But many will be vulnerable and it is the vulnerability of the class which provides the rationale for the law in question."

It concluded : "It is primarily for states to assess the risk and the likely incidence of abuse if the general prohibition on assisted suicides were relaxed or if exceptions were to be created."[1]

There was little, now, for the Court to add. Because "clear risks of abuse" did exist (sic), the Court, despite interference's only being justified in order to protect the vulnerable and despite seeing for itself that the applicant was not a vulnerable individual, left it to states to gauge the risk of abuse.

This "sacrificed" Mrs Pretty's legal autonomy by making the state the sole judge of the consequences, in her case, of making an exception to the inflexibility of the law.

The Court was, however, aware of the criticism that would inevitably be made – that it had not confined itself to its role as a court ruling on the facts of the case. In anticipatory reply, it said : "It is true that it is not this Court's role under Article 34 of the Convention to issue opinions in the abstract but to apply the Convention to the concrete facts of the individual case. However, judgments issued in individual cases establish precedents, albeit to a greater or lesser extent, and a decision in this case could not, either in theory or practice, be framed in such a way as to prevent application in later cases."[2]

Although, despite accepting that states had a wide margin of appreciation in the matter, the Court had found against Ireland for disproportionate interference which the Irish Government had justified on the grounds of protecting the right to life,[3] the Court preferred not to go down the same road here and allow even a tightly defined exception regarding end-of-life autonomy. This was probably because the sensitivity of the subject was here so great and because Ireland's particular position with respect to European positive law on abortion could not be compared with the United Kingdom's in the present case

1.
Ibid., paragraph 74.
2.
Ibid., paragraph 75.
3.
Open Door and Dublin Well Woman v. Ireland, judgment of 29 October 1992.

(of all the European countries covered by the ECHR, only the Netherlands and Belgium allow assisted suicide).

The solution adopted could therefore be justified as expedient and avoiding any radical departures despite the inconsistency of the reasoning and rejection of the appeal.

The second criticism is no less fundamental than the first since it disputes the Court's final conclusion. Noting that British law allowed a degree of flexibility in particular cases (consent was needed from the DPP to bring a prosecution, lesser penalties than the maximum sentence could be imposed, and in fact there had been only one conviction for murder in twenty-two cases between 1981 and 1992 concerned with "mercy killing"), it went on to say: "It does not appear to be arbitrary to the Court for the law to reflect the importance of the right to life, by prohibiting assisted suicide while providing for a system of enforcement and adjudication which allows due regard to be given in each particular case to the public interest in bringing a prosecution, as well as to the fair and proper requirements of retribution and deterrence."[1]

While one can follow the reasoning, one may nevertheless have some doubts as to the clarity of such a system in terms of legality of offences and penalties, but the Court did of course also reject the case for equal treatment in law when it examined the complaint under Article 14 combined with Article 8 of the ECHR.

Discrimination and the principle of autonomy at the end of life

Although there is a general prohibition on assisted suicide, did the applicant's physical disability which prevented her from ending her life without someone's assistance result in her being subjected to substantially different treatment amounting to discrimination?

The discrimination complained of consisted not in different treatment but in failure to take a difference into account in order to afford the applicant proper exercise of her right to autonomy.

In the Court's view, even if the principle that "[d]iscrimination may [...] arise where states without an objective and reasonable

1.
Pretty v. the United Kingdom, op. cit., paragraph 76.

justification fail to treat differently persons whose situations are significantly different" is applied, "there is [...] objective and reasonable justification for not distinguishing in law between those who are and those who are not physically capable of committing suicide".[1]

Reapplying the argument used to legitimise the interference under Article 8, paragraph 2, of the ECHR, the Court also concluded: "Similar reasons exist under Article 14 for not seeking to distinguish between those who are able and those who are unable to commit suicide unaided. The borderline between the two categories will often be a very fine one and to seek to build into the law an exemption for those judged to be incapable of committing suicide would seriously undermine the protection of life [...]."[2]

We need therefore go no further than the Court's general assertion that "the seriousness of the act for which immunity was claimed was such that the decision of the DPP to refuse the undertaking sought in the present case cannot be said to be arbitrary or unreasonable".[3]

The Pretty judgment is relevant to the question of the relationship between the right to life and euthanasia in several respects.

It establishes the special nature of the right to life under the ECHR as a right which, while placing positive obligations on states, can only be construed as a right to preservation of life because life, as a value guaranteed under Article 2 of the ECHR, is, like dignity and physical integrity, protected by the prohibition on torture, an (almost) absolute right.

For the first time – and this will take on growing significance – it accepts the principle of autonomy as a basis of the right to private life guaranteed in Article 8 and, within a broad, realistic conception of private life, it recognises the importance of choices concerning "quality of life" and, in the present case, the end of life. Nevertheless, it rejects the suggestion that, even if only for mentally competent, physically incapacitated individuals, assisted suicide may be included in the exercise of that

1.
Ibid., paragraph 89.

2.
Ibid., paragraph 89.

3.
Ibid., paragraph 77.

right. It leaves it entirely to states to decide how this right might be given a modicum of effectiveness. It approves the general and absolute line taken in the matter by national law but allows states some "flexibility" to decide – and this is the criticism made of the judgment – unilaterally and a posteriori how offences should be prosecuted and punished.

The fear of setting a precedent in a very sensitive social context under the media spotlight was clear. The Court sought to hold back, considering it appropriate to leave states a wide margin of appreciation in this area and finding that the respondent state had not "gone too far".

This has meant the important legal advances of the decision being (conveniently?) pushed into the background. Be that as it may, the Court's decisions – as the Court has itself said – do eventually become precedents.

References

Ariès, P., *L'homme devant la mort,* Paris, Le Seuil, 1977.

Kayser, P., *La Protection de la vie privée,* Paris, Marseilles, Economica et PVAM, 1990, p. 16.

Morin, E., *L'Homme et la mort,* Paris, Le Seuil, Coll. Point, 1976.

Prieur, S., *La Disposition par l'individu de son corps,* Bordeaux, Etudes Hospitalières, 1999.

Euthanasia
and religions

Buddhism

by Daniel Chevassut

Buddhism is practised all over the world. It originated in India
and, just as Japanese, Chinese, Vietnamese, Tibetan and other
forms of Buddhism emerged in the past, we are currently wit-
nessing the emergence of Western Buddhism.

While doing its best to preserve and treasure the authenticity
of Buddha's teaching, contemporary Buddhism must thus
adapt not only to Western culture but also to the changing
nature of multifaceted modern societies. Like other spiritual
traditions, it has to accept the impossibility of obtaining direct
answers from its founder. In days gone by, people put questions
to Buddha and Buddha replied. Today, practising Buddhists
confronting ethical issues must rely both on Buddha's teachings,
in so far as they have been preserved, and also on their own
experience shaped by direct application of the teachings.

With regard to ethical questions it is crucial to emphasise that
Buddhism has always given experience precedence over belief.
This also means that, in tackling difficult issues, it does not rely
solely on a specifically intellectual or analytical approach, but
also draws on the wisdom that stems from a clear view of reality.
Buddhism has been described as a metaphysical tradition
inspiring wisdom that is always applicable whatever the circumstances.[1] This wisdom lends it a naturally ethical dimension, expressed in the three traditional principles of Buddha's
teaching : listening to, studying and reflecting on what is
taught ; meditating ; and finally applying in one's everyday life
what one has understood, experienced and internalised in
these ways. The three principles may be compared to three
wheels of instruction. In essence, two aspects are fundamental
here : non-aggressiveness, which means doing no harm to
others, and the concept of interdependence, based on an
appreciation that one's own happiness is closely bound up
with the happiness of others.

1.
Ricard, M. and Revel,
J.F., *Le Moine et le
philosophe*, Paris, Nil
Editions, 1997.

Suffering, death and precious human life

The Buddhist path is based on establishing a healthy relationship with the realities of suffering and death – not in a pes-
simistic way but simply, on the one hand, because they are
unavoidable and, on the other, because Buddha offers, via the
path that he himself took, the possibility of liberation from all
types of suffering. This, incidentally, is the sense of the word
nirvana, meaning "extinction" (of all suffering).

Another important concept in attempting to grasp the Buddhist
perspective on euthanasia is that of the preciousness of human
life. Buddhists believe that attaining human form is extremely
difficult. Encountering the teaching of Buddha (the *dharma*)
and having the opportunity of putting it into practice is rarer
still – "as rare as stars in the sky at dawn or dusk", as a traditional saying puts it. One must, to begin with, be born a human
being, live in a country where Buddha's teachings are accessi-
ble, have enough to eat, enjoy freedom and possess a body and
mind that lend themselves to spiritual practice. These factors
together confer precious human life.

For Buddhists, therefore, human life is especially important
and this applies particularly to the time before death, a time
that can bring spiritual growth, provided of course that one
has been a life-long practitioner and that one's clinical condition
is not an impediment. For a practising Buddhist this is a vital
juncture.

The euthanasia question

In accordance with Buddha's teaching, the question of
euthanasia, like any other ethical or bioethical question, has to
be addressed first and foremost in a spirit of openness, goodwill, compassion, wisdom and non-aggressiveness. These are
essential if we are to avoid an overly rigid or legalistic
approach.

To put it simply, the Buddhist vision of the end of life is very
close to current thinking in the palliative care movement, with
the emphasis on comforting the dying and easing their suffering
as much as possible. What is important, as one teacher puts it,

is to respect life just as much as we respect the views of the patient.[1] This represents a type of "middle way" between artificially prolonging life and euthanasia, and involves little or no aggression. Each case is seen as special and the circumstances of each terminally ill patient must be considered individually, in order to preserve an essential margin of discretion. Three questions need to be asked:

– What is the person's real overall situation (in physical, psychological, spiritual, social and other terms)?

– What is the true nature of the request (since many requests for euthanasia stem from excessive suffering, often not properly alleviated)?

– What proper – namely, appropriate – responses are possible, given not only the patient's situation and the fact of the request, but also the care skills, the hospital's resources and, ultimately, each carer's own sense of ethics?

From this perspective, Buddhism is opposed to any change in the law that would permit euthanasia, inasmuch as such a move could well open the way to abuses of all types, occasioning much suffering. The current debate on euthanasia would seem to reflect shortcomings in the treatment of suffering at the end of life, and a certain inflexibility in the law, rather than the existence of a definite pro-euthanasia lobby. More work is needed to improve our ability to understand, assess and treat difficult symptoms such as certain types of pain, dyspnoea and anxiety. Research is as essential in the field of terminal illness and palliative care as in any other discipline. There is also a basic need for the medical world, and society generally, to recognise that the end of life is a precious time for human beings. As Buddhists see it, this dimension is insufficiently emphasised, and this particular time of our lives deserves our concentrated attention.

Moreover, given the huge responsibility borne by decision makers in such situations, the wise approach would seem to be the collective one already practised in some hospitals, involving the whole medical team and, of course, the patient and family. Certainly the decision to terminate life must never be taken in isolation, but rather in association with the hospital

1.
Lama Denys Teundroup.

team and the family, and with reference to the patient's own wishes. In cases where the patient is in a coma, it is important to know as much as possible – in terms of both diagnosis and appropriate therapy – about the particular pathology and the various possible outcomes. There is no substitute for the information the family can supply about the patient's wishes and character. And the carers themselves need emotional support. Experience has shown just how draining and destabilising daily contact with suffering can be.

Ultimately, from a Buddhist point of view, the first requirement in dealing with a request for euthanasia is open-mindedness, taking account not only of the patient's wishes but also of his or her actual circumstances and environment (both human and material). Basic to this is a care climate of love, serenity, compassion and wisdom, something that doctors, nurses and other carers have to work at individually and collectively in an appropriately supportive context and that it takes great motivation to achieve. As Vercors[1] put it, humanity is not a condition to be passively undergone but a dignity to be actively striven for.

Catholicism

by Gabriella Gambino

The Catholic Church has always been especially attentive to the theological and pastoral problems surrounding euthanasia as a bioethical question with major social and personal implications. Particularly in the latter half of the twentieth century, it spoke out on the issue with frequent statements by Popes Pius XII,[1] Paul VI[2] and John Paul II and, in 1980, publication by the Sacred Congregation for the Doctrine of the Faith of the *Declaration on euthanasia* – "Iura et bona", which has remained one of the key doctrinal pronouncements on the subject. The declaration sets out a number of fundamental principles which the Church, as it has evolved, considers to be definitive and universally applicable : the acknowledgement that human life is God's creation and is sacred ; the primacy of the individual in relation to society ; and the duty of those in authority to respect human life.[3] These same principles were confirmed in 1995 in Pope John Paul II's encyclical *Evangelium vitae* and confirmation has also come from numerous doctrinal texts by bishops the world over.[4]

The Catholic Church has developed its teachings so as to (a) clarify and differentiate between the various concepts relating to euthanasia and (b) broaden the debate to take in different forms of euthanasia, including neonatal euthanasia[5] and social euthanasia,[6] while setting out the Christian community's duty of appropriate support to the dying. In Catholic doctrine the strict definition of euthanasia is "an action or an omission which, of itself or by intention, causes death, in order that all suffering may in this way be eliminated".[7] In euthanasia, the key points are thus the intention of the will and the methods used. The Church's moral judgment on euthanasia is clear and categorical :

> "[...] nothing and no one can in any way permit the killing of an innocent human being, whether a foetus or an embryo, an infant or an adult, an old person, or one suffering from an incurable disease, or a person who is dying. Furthermore, no one is permitted to ask for this act of killing, either for himself or herself or for another person entrusted to his or her care,

nor can he or she consent to it, either explicitly or implicitly. Nor can any authority legitimately recommend or permit such an action. For it is a question of the violation of the divine law, an offence against the dignity of the human person, a crime against life, and an attack on humanity."[8]

"This doctrine is based upon the natural law and upon the written word of God, is transmitted by the Church's Tradition[9] and taught by the ordinary and universal Magisterium."[10] The same condemnation has been restated in respect of suicide and what is termed "assisted suicide".[11] For Christians, the rejection of euthanasia and suicide is grounded in faith and hope in Christ, who, through his suffering and resurrection, brought new meaning to human existence and human suffering – as a possible source of good if it is experienced for love and with love, through sharing in the suffering of Christ Crucified.[12]

The Church makes a distinction between euthanasia and "the decision to forego […] 'aggressive medical treatment', in other words, medical procedures which no longer correspond to the real situation of the patient, either because they are by now disproportionate to any expected results or because they impose an excessive burden on the patient and his family, […] so long as the normal care due to the sick person in similar cases is not interrupted".[13] "To forego […] disproportionate means is not the equivalent of suicide or euthanasia ; it rather expresses acceptance of the human condition in the face of death."[14] In any event, decisions in such situations must be guided by the principle of proportionality of treatment. It is also permissible, with the patient's consent, to use new and even experimental methods, provided they are not dangerous.

The right to death with dignity – a topical concept today – must not therefore mean the right to procure death, or have it procured, in the manner one wishes, but rather the right to die in all serenity with human and Christian dignity.[15] Here, the Church sees palliative care as playing a particularly important role. One of the issues in this area is the legitimacy of using various types of analgesics and sedatives to relieve pain if they carry the risk of shortening the patient's life. Pope Pius XII stated that the use of narcotics to alleviate pain was legitimate

– even if they had the effect of reducing consciousness and shortening life – "if no other means exist".[16] In such cases, death is not willed or sought: it is a risk taken for reasonable motives, from a desire to ease pain effectively by using the analgesics which medicine provides. All the same, it is not right to deprive the dying person of consciousness without a serious reason: as death approaches, there are moral, family and religious duties which people need to be able to attend to.[17] Thus the priority must always be to establish dialogue with patients and keep them informed. Lastly, the Church has made the point that the occasional death pleas from gravely ill people are not to be understood as implying a true desire for euthanasia but almost always as indirect pleas not merely for appropriate medical care but for more attention and interest from those around them. "The sick person who feels surrounded by a loving human and Christian presence does not give way to depression and anguish as would be the case if one were left to suffer and die alone and wanting to be done with life. This is why euthanasia is a defeat for the one who proposes it, decides it and carries it out."[18]

References

1. Pope Pius XII, encyclical *Mystici corporis,* 29 June 1943 ; address to the Italian Medico-Biological Union of St Luke, 1944 ; address to the 1st International Congress on Histopathology of the Nervous System, 14 September 1952 ; address to the 7th Congress of Catholic Doctors, 11 September 1956 ; address to the Catholic Union of Obstetricians, 29 October 1951 ; address to the 9th Congress of the Italian Anaesthesiological Society, 24 February 1957 ; and address to the International Congress of the Collegium Internationale Neuropsychopharmacologicum, 9 September 1958.

2. Pope Paul VI, address to the International College of Psychosomatic Medicine, 18 September 1975.

3. The Catholic Church sees protection of human life as having a secular and rational basis : it has been defined by Pope Pius XII as a natural right and by the Sacred Congregation for the Doctrine of the Faith as a fundamental human right.

4. Pontifical Council "Cor Unum", "Ethical questions concerning the seriously ill and the dying", 27 June 1981 ; letter on public morality by the Bishops of England and Wales, 31 December 1970 ; communiqué of the Episcopate of Panama, 23 November 1974 ; statement by the Bishops of Mexico on respect for human life, 8 September 1975 ; letter from the Bishops of Rwanda, 31 May 1975 ; statement by the East German Episcopate, 1 June 1975 ; pastoral letter from the Irish Bishops, 1 May 1975 ; Secretariat of the French Episcopal Conference, "Problèmes éthiques posés aujourd'hui par la mort et le mourir", *Bulletin du Secrétariat de la Conférence Episcopale Française,* 6 March 1976 ; statement by the German Episcopal Conference of 20 November 1978 on dignified death and Christian death ; Spanish Episcopal Conference on La eutanasia. 100 cuestiones y respuestas sobre la defensa de la vida y la actitud de los catòlicos, Madrid, 1993 ; Catholic Bishops of Florida, pastoral statement on "Life, death and the treatment of dying patients", *Medicina e Morale,* 3, 1990, pp. 618-624 ; Standing Council of the French Episcopal Conference, statement entitled "Respecter l'homme proche de sa mort", *Medicina e Morale,* 1, 1992, pp. 124-133 ; Pope John Paul II, address to the International Congress on Care of the Dying (17 March 1992), *Medicina e Morale,* 3, 1992, pp. 419-422 ; Belgian Episcopal Conference on L'accompagnement des personnes à l'approche de la mort, 1994 ; Belgian Episcopal Conference, statement entitled "L'Euthanasie : un pas en arrière pour la civilisation", June 2001 ; Belgian Episcopal Conference on *Soins palliatifs, oui ; Euthanasie, non !,* 16 May 2002 ; and Catholic Bishops of Illinois, pastoral letter "Facing the end of life", *Medicina e Morale,* 4, 2002, pp. 758-763. The Assembly

of the Pontifical Academy for Life recently devoted one of its general meetings to the theme of euthanasia (see Dios Vial Correa de, J. and Sgreccia, E. (eds.), *The dignity of the dying person,* proceedings of the fifth Assembly of the Pontifical Academy for Life, Vatican City, 24 to 27 February 1999, Vatican City, Libreria Editrice Vaticana, 2000), and on 9 December 2000 it published the document *Respect for the dignity of the dying,* setting out ethical considerations on euthanasia.

Almost all the magisterium documents quoted here can be found on the Vatican website : http ://www.vatican.va

5. Pope Pius XII, encyclical *Mystici corporis,* 29 June 1943.

6. Pontifical Academy for Life, *Respect for the dignity of the dying,* No. 4, 9 December 2000.

7. Pope John Paul II, encyclical *Evangelium vitae,* No. 65, 25 March 1995. See also Sacred Congregation for the Doctrine of the Faith, *Declaration on euthanasia* – "Iura et bona", No. 2, 5 May 1980 ; Visser, J.V., "Pronunciamento ufficiale della S. Sede sull'eutanasia", *Medicina e Morale,* 3, 1981, pp. 358-372.

8. Sacred Congregation for the Doctrine of the Faith, *Declaration on euthanasia* – "Iura et bona", No. 2.

9. Second Vatican Council, Pastoral Constitution *Gaudium et spes,* No. 27.

10. *Evangelium vitae,* No. 65 ; and Second Vatican Council, Dogmatic Constitution, *Lumen gentium,* No. 25.

11. *Catechism of the Catholic Church,* Nos. 2281-2283.

12. *Evangelium vitae,* No. 67.

13. Between artificial prolonging of life on the one hand and palliative care on the other, it is thus important to distinguish what constitutes "ordinary" care, including the supply of food and fluids, to which every patient is entitled, for suspending such care can effectively amount to euthanasia. See Catholic Bishops of Pennsylvania, "Nutrition and hydration : moral considerations", *Medicina e Morale,* 1992, 4, pp. 739-763 ; and statement of the United States Bishops' Pro-Life Committee, "Nutrition and hydration : moral and pastoral considerations", *Medicina e Morale,* 4, 1992, pp. 763-783.

14. *Evangelium vitae,* No. 65 and *Declaration on euthanasia* – "Iura et bona", No. 4.

15. *Declaration on euthanasia* – Iura et bona, Nos. 3-4.

16. Pope Pius XII, address to an international group of doctors, 24 February 1957.

17. *Evangelium vitae,* No. 65.

18. Pontifical Council for Pastoral Assistance to Health Care Workers, *The Charter for Health Care Workers,* No. 149, Vatican City, 1995.

Islam

by Raoutsi Hadj Eddine Sari Ali

Life of the soul or life of the body?

In today's great international debates about bioethics, we come up against the general problem of what "life" means. There is no doubt that, since the Enlightenment, the Western world, and Europe in particular, has been a powerhouse of progress in every field of science. Western medicine has conquered the devastating ills that once decimated the population. Although, in Europe and elsewhere, the Darwinist proposition of humanity's descent from the apes offended Christian thinking, it did not provoke militant ethical counter-reactions. But the response to biotechnology (in the case of removing organs from the dying, for example), and to medically assisted procreation, has been quite different. For Christians, Jews and Muslims, human life is meaningful only as the life of the soul – *nefs* in Arabic, *nefesh* in Hebrew – and a semantic ambiguity thus arises, for believers take bioethics to be ethics of the life of the soul. Neurologists have never claimed to be in the business of addressing or explaining the concept of the soul, while theologians, who are not biologists, reject the reduction of the human being to a set of physio-chemical phenomena. Even Teilhard de Chardin was censured by his peers for seeking to ally science and theology. In the Islamic world, Avicenna, Rhazes and Averroës had to battle to promote an understanding of bodily illnesses as distinct from the vicissitudes of the soul.

Euthanasia is foreign to the Islamic view of humankind

It was in 1771 that the term "euthanasia" first made its appearance in Europe. The idea of procuring a gentle death for one's fellow human being in order to prevent unnecessary suffering was the culmination of a long process in Western philosophy. The modern hedonism of the eighteenth century, as promoted by Jeremy Bentham, was the philosophy of utilitarianism. Bentham, who called himself a renovator of Christianity, argued that Saint Paul's teachings were at odds with those of Christ, who was the true originator of utilitarianism. Today, the whole weight of ethical thinking appears to favour an acceptance that human beings are animals, that they lead the same kind of lives as animals and die as animals die, and that it is thus legitimate to kill them in order to cut short their suffering – just as horses are put down when they are no longer able to race. In Islam, the Koran humanises animals : there are animal nations just as there are human nations, and humankind is expected to take its example from them, even in matters of morality.[1]

Jewish, Christian and Muslim believers have systematically rejected the notion of euthanasia : Jews and Christians base their opposition on respect for the sacredness of human life. For Muslims, euthanasia stands in contradiction to the practice of medicine : they believe that only the Creator has the power to call back the soul (or *nefs*) ; the secondary causes of death – illness, accidents, disasters – fall within the authority of His vicar *(khalifa)* on Earth,[2] whose responsibility it is to combat them.[3] For the Muslim believer, euthanasia – the giving of death – is thus unthinkable on both religious and rational grounds.

Death is merely a personal transition natural to every creature

"Every soul must taste of death [...] Allah takes men's souls at the time of their death and those that die not, during their sleep. Then he withholds those on whom he has passed the decree of death and sends the others back till an appointed term."[4] In one *hadyth,* or tradition, of Islam, the prophet teaches that martyrs – *chouhada* – include victims of incurable diseases, disasters, injustice or wars, as well as women who die in childbirth. In cases where medicine cannot offer any cure, the proper attitude is to consign the patient to the hands of God *(Islam)*, while continuing to provide active care, for suffering is not inevitable. God created the disease, the remedy and the cure – *da, dawa, shifa.* Hence there is a human responsibility to identify the disease, seek out the remedy and provide nursing care. The doctor who evades that responsibility under the pretext of compassion is regarded in the same light as the soldier who runs away from battle because he fears death. Muslim

1.
Koran, VI/38 and V/31.

2.
Ibid., VIII/23, XIV/10, XXXV/32, LXI/5, II/30, VI/165, XXV/39, VII/12.

3.
Ibid., III/47 to 51, V/110.

4.
Ibid., III/185, XXI/35, XXIX/57 and XXXIX/42.

doctors will therefore go to much greater lengths than others to prolong life – short of turning their patients into guinea pigs – because, for them, the option of palliative care is second best. External signs of bodily suffering must receive medical attention; believers cannot accept the concept of quality-adjusted life-years (QALYs), which weighs age alongside factors such as financial resources and quantification of pain. That is how decisions on whether to administer euthanasia are currently reached. In the Islamic system of medical ethics, each patient is unique in the face of death and no generalisations are possible. What affects each individual in his or her time on earth cannot be evaluated by anyone else.[1] When a fellow human being is sick, believers will arm themselves with patience and try to do good,[2] without discrimination on religious or other grounds, and fearing neither death nor illness.[3] The writings of Misk-awayh and others emphasise that human beings are led astray by conjecture: they are given to precipitateness *(ajl)*, particularly when confronted by suffering, but no one is infallible and no one has life-and-death authority over another.[4] Even if patients plead for death, it is the doctor's duty to relieve their suffering and not accede to suicide requests.[5]

When we analyse texts advocating the legitimacy of euthanasia we find two major arguments: one economic, the other based on the right to dignity in death. From the standpoint of Islamic ethics, economic considerations have no place whatever as an argument for discontinuing or refusing treatment. With regard to dignity in death, we learn from the example of Job[6] and from Jesus' attitude to the lepers that we should not abandon a suffering person on grounds of compassion: Job's wife surrounded him with affection to the best of her ability, she did not bring about his death despite his suffering, and she reminded him of his faith in God; Jesus embraced the lepers, thus according them their dignity. What is regrettable is that states should believe they can override the collective sense of right and wrong by passing laws that reify humankind and the human conscience. All in all, in the eyes of Islam, passive euthanasia is an abuse, and active euthanasia a crime.

1.
Ibid., VI/94 to 98, XX/107, XIX/80 to 95, and XVII/13 to 15 and 84 to 85.

2.
Ibid., XI/11 and VI/150 to 153.

3.
Ibid., XVII/85 and II/285.

4.
Ibid., XVII/76, XVII/85 and XLV/18 to 26.

5.
Ibid., LXXIV/11 to 23 and 38.

6.
The story of Job in the Koran is ethically opposite to the Bible version in which Job's wife drives him to hate God and to kill himself. For the Koranic version quoted see Sura IV, verse 163 and Sura XXI, verses 83 to 90.

Bibliography

Emir Abdelkader, *Ecrits spirituels,* Paris, Le Seuil, 1969.

Avicenna, *Poème de la médecine,* Paris, Les Belles Lettres, 1956.

Boukhari, *Le recueil des traditions authentiques,* Paris, Maisonneuve, 1970.

Changeux, J.P., *L'Homme neuronal,* Paris, Pluriel, 1984.

Parekh, B., *Critical assessment,* London, Routledge, 1993.

Teilhard de Chardin, P., *Le Phénomène humain,* Le Seuil, 1970.

Miskawayh's ethics, translated into French by Arkoun, M., Damascus, Institut français, 1967.

N.B. Recommended translations of the Koran (into French) : Cheikh Hamza Boubakeur, Fayard or Muhammad Hamidullah, Edition Les Belles Lettres. English edition consulted for translation of this article into English, Muhammad Ali, M., *The holy Qur'an : Arabic text, English translation and commentary,* Lahore, Ahmadiyya Anjuman, 1951.

Judaism

by Albert Guigui

In Judaism, respect for human life is absolute, sacred and inviolable. The life of a human being cannot be measured or weighed. Each second of a life has an absolute value. A single moment in a life is invested with unparalleled importance because it takes only a moment of full repentance to effect the transformation from iniquity to rectitude.[1]

Human life is of infinite value because we are made in God's image. "Therefore man was created singly to teach you that whoever destroys a single life is considered by Scripture as if he had destroyed an entire world, and that whoever preserves a life is considered by Scripture as if he had preserved an entire world."[2]

The great importance placed on protecting life inevitably affects religious practice. Certain religious prescriptions are adapted or overridden when life is in danger. For example, the importance of the Sabbath as a day of rest is well known, but it is permissible, and indeed a duty, to break the rule of resting on the Sabbath day, and even to break other commandments, for the purpose of saving a human life.[3] Similarly, Yom Kippur, the Day of Atonement, is one of the most sacred days in the Hebrew calendar, a day when it is forbidden (among other things) to work or to eat food of any kind. Yet if life is in danger, it is permissible to give a sick person as much food as he or she requires.[4]

Against this background it is easy to see why the concept of euthanasia provokes opposition from traditional Jewish thinkers. Judaism rejects the idea of terminating life, even through a compassionate desire to end the suffering of the very ill.

Hebrew law opposes any form of decriminalisation of euthanasia. The *Shulchan Aruch* code of Jewish law stipulates unequivocally that a person who is dying is to be regarded as a living person in all respects. It is forbidden to intervene in any way that could hasten death. In Jewish tradition the situation of the

1.
See Gugenheim, E.,
Les Portes de la loi,
Paris, Albin Michel,
1982, p. 249.

2.
Babylonian Talmud,
Sanhedrin, 37.a.

3.
Yoma, 92.a.

4.
Orah Hayyim, 617.2.

dying person is likened to the flickering flame of a candle, extinguished as soon as it is touched.[1] The Torah makes no distinction in this respect between children, with their whole lives in front of them, and the very old.

Legalising euthanasia could pave the way for all types of abuses. The term "mercy killing" is used, but mercy is an ambiguous concept. Compassion towards the sick often masks conscious or unconscious motives that are not rooted in mercy alone.[2] Sometimes, financial considerations can find expression under the cover of mercy. There is a risk that insistence by some in authority on curbing health service spending could result in legislation permitting "euthanasia on economic grounds", with the poor and destitute as the first victims.

Artificial prolonging of life rejected

While Judaism forbids euthanasia, doctors do have a duty to alleviate their patients' physical and mental suffering by all means available to them. Judaism invites us to respond actively to others' misfortune and to offer support. There can be no excuse for refusing to act when confronted by suffering.

There is no moral obligation to prolong life by artificial means. Helping a patient to survive is a duty, but using medication or sophisticated equipment to prolong the survival of a dying person whose vital functions are fatally impaired is a feat of science and by no means an act of humanity.

The *Shulchan Aruch* explains Judaism's position as follows: "If there is anything which causes a hindrance to the departure of the soul [...] then it is permissible to remove [it]." Such cases do not entail any action that directly hastens death, but simply removing the hindrance without any disturbance to the dying person.[3]

Judaism defends the individual's right to die with dignity, in an atmosphere of calm and peace, without futile recourse to the latest medical technology. In every case, the patient must be supplied with the basic elements that sustain all human life.[4] The development of clinics specialising in palliative care thus seems an appropriate solution.

1.
Yoreh De'ah, 339.1.

2.
Psychiatrist Henri Baruk makes the point that the word "euthanasia" translates into Hebrew as *hamatat hessed* (mercy killing). However, the Hebrew word *hessed* has two meanings: "mercy", but also "opprobrium" or excessive, ill-considered compassion. According to the rabbis of the Talmud, the sentiment of mercy or compassion must be underpinned by a concern for truth - an idea encapsulated in the traditional Hebrew expression *hessed ve émeth* (mercy and truth).

3.
Yoreh De'ah, 339.1.

4.
These include food and hydration via drip or feeding tube, oxygen and possibly blood transfusions.

Judaism

The great majority of rabbis do not take the view that suffering is valuable for its own sake. It is our duty to combat suffering. And it is precisely the wide range of medical resources now available for pain relief that renders legislation on euthanasia unnecessary. In fact, this is a field in which legislation becomes dangerous, for experience has shown that, in countries which have euthanasia laws, abuses are rife. To quote Montesquieu : "If it is not necessary to make a law, it is necessary not to make a law."

The way forward is by no means easy. Sensitive to the dual tradition of respecting life and relieving the suffering of others, we must attempt to take the difficult path that allows both duties to be realised in situations such as those described, where the contradiction between them is evident. We must place our trust in doctors, whose vocation it is to ease pain and to combat sickness and death. Jewish ethics offers no obvious "right path", no open door. At best it offers to help light our way through a darkness in which suffering, solitude and death could befall us at any moment.

Orthodox Church[1]

by Alexandre M. Stavropoulos

The stance of Orthodox theology on euthanasia is based as much on the study of life, death and eternity as on the meaning of suffering and tribulation in human lives. The Orthodox Church's categorical rejection of euthanasia derives from the perception of it as arbitrary human intervention, for our lives are a supreme gift from God and their beginning and end are in His hands alone.[2] Each person's life is, moreover, the space in which his or her freedom finds expression and in which the grace of God meets the human will in achieving salvation of the individual. All human intervention in the course of life constitutes a rejection not only of God's work but also of that dimension of life that is concerned with salvation through redemption.

The Church preaches the immortality of the soul, the resurrection of the body and the hope and reality of eternity. In the Orthodox tradition, the approach to the end of life is a time – like periods of weakness, suffering and ordeal – imbued with a hidden sacredness that merits special respect on the part of families, doctors, carers and society as a whole. In many cases, these special times induce a more spiritual attitude to life. From this standpoint, the dying person's suffering and tribulation are interpreted as "the marks of the Lord Jesus" in the body[3] and as occasions of salvation. Any death that occurs as a result of human decisions and choices – however "good" an end it might be – is rejected as an insult to God. Any medical procedure intended to precipitate death rather than prolong life is viewed as unethical and bringing the medical profession into disrepute.

According to the Fathers of the Church, the reality of pain in human life, like every trial that individuals undergo, assists the salvation of the believer and, in some cases, can be "more profitable" than health itself. Of course, recognising the weakness of human nature, the Church, with unfailing charity, prays for deliverance "from all tribulation, wrath, danger and necessity" and, on occasions, for the repose of those suffering on the brink of death. In the Orthodox faith, people are required to pray, not to take life-or-death decisions. Indeed, every holy

1.
The views outlined in this article are a synthesis of those recently formulated by the Holy Synod of the Church in Greece and publicised there when European governments were adopting positions on the question. They are based on the biblical, patristic and liturgical tradition of the Orthodox Church. It should be noted that what Orthodox believers call a "Christian end", in the sense used in our Church's prayer, was termed "euthanasia" by the Ancient Greeks. The word "euthanasia" never meant the premature end of a life of unjust suffering nor the end of a desperate, unhappy life, and was never used in a sense comparable to the current one of "supporting" a person into death.

2.
Job xii.10.

3.
Galatians vi.17.

liturgy includes a prayer of the faithful "for a Christian end to our lives, peaceful, without shame and suffering".

Today, theologians and members of the Orthodox clergy take serious issue with the "right to die", which is the *de facto* legal defence for euthanasia. They voice their opposition openly because this is a practice that could escalate to threaten the lives of patients unable to afford treatment and hospitalisation. One view expressed today is that the current concepts of dignity in death and passive assistance with death on grounds of compassion actually reflect the fact that love of God, faith in God and love and trust for our fellow human beings are in decline and have been superseded by utilitarianism and logic.

Euthanasia, from the standpoint of the Orthodox faith, although justified by some today as an entitlement to "death with dignity", in reality constitutes assisted suicide – that is, murder and suicide combined. Christians have a duty to show proper respect for the human body from the moment it is created to the hour of its natural death because it is "the temple of the Holy Ghost which is in you, which ye have of God".[1] Therefore, "if any man defile the temple of God, him shall God destroy";[2] moreover, it is in the body that God's glory and incorruptibility are preserved, following the Resurrection, as the Apostle Paul explained : "But if the Spirit of him that raised up Jesus from the dead dwell in you, he that raised up Christ from the dead shall also quicken your mortal bodies by his Spirit that dwelleth in you."[3]

The approach of death has the potential to promote reconciliation, the development of a society based on love and the expression of pity. When certain patients request euthanasia, they are, at bottom, questioning their families' love for them and their own desire to be with their families. Orthodox theologians would regard as unilateralist (and racist) a society that turned itself into a pitiless power interested only in the healthy and strong and directing all others towards a so-called dignified death. On the contrary, the values that need to be fostered are those of love and respect for every human being, irrespective of race or religion, from the moment of conception until the hour of death.

1.
I Corinthians vi.19.

2.
I Corinthians iii.17.

3.
Romans viii.11.

To sum up, the Orthodox Church's main tenets on euthanasia which it would hope to see reflected in the drafting of the European Union's new constitution for the twenty-first century are as follows:

- human life is a gift from God and Jesus Christ, who was crucified and resurrected for all our sakes;
- contrary to any claims about dignity, euthanasia can be deemed a decadent phenomenon in society inasmuch as it is contemptuous of human beings;
- the Orthodox Church emphasises the existential dimension of pain, illness and imminent death. It takes the view that everything the individual undergoes is profitable and that no one is entitled to adjust or interfere with God's plan;
- the Orthodox Church approaches death with respect because it constitutes the beginning of a new mode of existence. The Church's own offer of "euthanasia" is that of faith in eternal life as a means of overcoming death.

Protestantism

by Jean-François Collange

In matters of ethics, Protestantism makes no claim to possess truths. It attempts, by offering a series of ideas, to clarify the thinking of men and women who wish to use its values as points of reference and to get involved in the process of debate that is essential to any society seeking guidelines for its development. Protestantism sees its function as the shaping of individual and collective conscience, and in this way it aims to stimulate and advance debate, and to encourage people to speak out and assume responsibility in all its forms.

It is from this perspective that the question of euthanasia has been addressed in recent years. Christianity in general, and indeed Western society as a whole, has traditionally regarded the taking of another's life, in whatever circumstances, as murder and thus as unacceptable. Protestantism has endorsed this unanimous view, all the more so since it rejected with horror the aberrations of the Nazi era in this regard.

None the less, progress in medical technology and various technological means of artificially prolonging life, the shift within medicine from paternalism to acknowledgment of patient autonomy, and the increasing attention devoted to suffering at the end of life have combined to put euthanasia, as an ethical question, on the public agenda.

In 1991 a proposal to legalise euthanasia came before the European Parliament, and this led the ethics committee of the Fédération Protestante de France (French Protestant Federation) to take a stance on the issue. A few years later the Evangelische Kirche in Deutschland (Protestant Church in Germany) also spoke out on the subject.

These two positions – followed by the opinion of the Protestant churches of the Netherlands – are outlined below as examples of European Protestant thinking on the question.

Euthanasia and assisting the dying: Fédération Protestante de France (FPF) (1991)[1]

In 1991, the ethics committee of the Fédération Protestante de France was not prepared to countenance legalisation of

1.
See *Livre blanc de la commission d'éthique*, Fédération protestante de France, 47 rue de Clichy, F-75009 Paris.

euthanasia. It rejected various arguments advanced by those advocating a "right to die with dignity". Dignity was not a measurable commodity and it was not possible to fix a dignity threshold. Moreover, people could not accord or deny themselves dignity, it was something accorded, in every case, by others. "In our eyes, dignity is the fact of being created in God's image. That is why no one can appropriate dignity and no one (not even the churches) can dictate what constitutes dignity." The fédération also repudiated the concept of control over death : "[...] what we find disturbing about euthanasia is the presumption that one can assume full charge of oneself, remaining the active agent of one's life right through to death, and turning death into an active step or a decision (rather than something that one undergoes or encounters). Despite appearances, euthanasia in this sense is a mirror image of the artificial prolonging of life to which it is opposed : it constitutes the same type of activism, with human beings refusing their own limitations and seeking to remain in control."

The important thing, therefore, was to promote and develop palliative care, which ultimately enabled people to look death in the face, offered a means of supporting them right to the end and considerably alleviated their suffering.

At the same time, recognising that, in a very few cases, suffering persists despite all efforts, the statement went on to say that "some Protestants feel there is a request that must be heard, expressing not a desire to end it all, but rather a plea on the part of the dying person that his or her remaining time should not be interminably eroded by pain and degeneration [...] it is not up to us to pass judgment here [...], particularly as the dying person, in making the request, is neither judging nor deciding anything – but merely asking for death. For the person concerned, death is not an active step : it means consenting to something outside oneself, accepting that one can love oneself as one would a family member."

"Life to the very end: dying as a part of life" (1996) and "The end of life in a spirit of love" (2002): Protestant Church in Germany[1]

The first of the German texts dates from 1996 and, in keeping with its title – "Life to the very end" – makes no mention of euthanasia. It reads as a powerful argument for palliative care

1.
See "Arbeitsfelder, Texte" at http://www.ekd.de
More recently, in 2002, the Protestant Church in Germany again spoke out on the issue in a much longer document dealing with many of the current challenges in bioethics : *Im Geist der Liebe mit dem Leben umgehen - Argumentationshilfe für aktuelle medizin- und bioethische Fragen* (Dealing with life in a spirit of love : an aid to debate on current questions of biomedical ethics), EKD-Texte 71, 2002, point 3.2 "Lebensende". Hard-copy versions of these documents may be obtained from the head office of the EKD (Protestant Church in Germany), Herren-häuser Straße 12, D-30419 Hanover.

Protestantism

and for the development in Germany of the hospice movement, as originated in the UK. Assessing what it means to die in this day and age, it deplores the fact that death is increasingly evaded and, as it were, rejected. Hence the need to follow the Bible's example by making death a part of life in its own right. Yet living also means being close to others, allowing others to be close to us, exchanging with others and bearing witness to the fact that, even beyond death, lies the hope of life conquering death, through Jesus Christ. It is in this spirit of life and love *(Geist der Liebe)* – a spirit to which many people are led through Christian faith – that initiatives for the development of palliative care should be promoted, and Christians should be encouraged to support them actively.

The second document, published six years later, emphasises the same points. But it also acknowledges the increasingly vocal demand for the right to die with dignity. In this context, the written expression of the patient's wishes can be of great assistance to doctors. There is a willingness to contemplate alleviating excessive suffering even at the risk of hastening death *(indirekte Sterbehilfe),* but not actively causing death. Obviously, the distinction between active and passive euthanasia is not always clear-cut, yet it must be maintained because it reflects a fundamental Christian theme which pervades our culture : the idea that death must be awaited or encountered ("abwarten" is the German word used), rather than provoked. At the same time, the contradictions of the human condition are evident in a number of cases. It is thus not impossible that doctors will find themselves in borderline situations in this connection – although the text leaves open the question of whether legislation should specifically deal with such situations. While not ignoring the case for clarifying what is currently a grey area, the document strikes a very cautious note here. It suggests that any provision in law for euthanasia would breach what has so far been a solid edifice, just as placing too much weight on the notion of individual autonomy could have grave psychological and social repercussions. Once again, the alternative way would thus seem to lie in the development of palliative care.

It is clear that in both France and Germany principles have been robustly expounded and defended, and palliative care has been promoted, although developments are apparent and extreme situations are taken into account. In this context,

155

mention has to be made of the position taken by the majority of Protestant churches in the Netherlands on the Dutch legislation permitting euthanasia. While raising no objections of substance, the churches complain about shortcomings in the way that the law is applied.

Appendices

Appendix I – Some key concepts

Euthanasia

The term "euthanasia" comes from the Ancient Greek "eu" – good, and "thanatos" – death, therefore meaning a peaceful, painless death. It refers to procedures used in cases of terminal illness to spare the patient a protracted death or extreme pain.

In practice, euthanasia can take several forms:

- active euthanasia is the intentional administration of lethal substances with the intention of ending life, either at the patient's request or, without the patient's consent, by decision of a close relative or the medical profession;

- in assisted suicide, it is the patient who ends his or her own life, aided by another person who provides the necessary information or means. The term "medically assisted suicide" is used where the patient ends his or her own life by orally or intravenously taking drugs prescribed and provided by a doctor;

- indirect euthanasia is administration of analgesics resulting in death as an unintentional side effect;

- passive euthanasia is the withholding or withdrawal of treatment necessary to sustain life.

Palliative care

The WHO (2000) defines palliative care as "an approach which improves the quality of life of patients and their families facing life-threatening illness, through the prevention, assessment and treatment of pain and other physical, psychosocial and spiritual problems."

Appendix II – A selection of useful websites

http://www.ccne-ethique.fr/
Site of the French National Consultative Ethics Committee for Health and Life Sciences (English translation available). See in particular Opinion No. 63, "Fin de vie, arrêt de vie, euthanasie" (End of life, ending life, euthanasia).

http://www.senat.fr/
Site of the French Senate (limited English translation available). Select the heading "Europe and international", click on "Europe" then go to "Comparative legislation studies". See, notably, Study LC 109 (2002) (not available in translation) on euthanasia in seven countries, supplementing Study LC 49 (1999).

http://www.genethique.org/
Forum (in French) for debate on bioethics. Dossiers available on euthanasia and palliative care, in addition to several articles, official documents and other information on the subject.

http://www.hospice-spc-council.org.uk/
Site of an association specialising in palliative care.

http://www.euthanasia.com/
Information on euthanasia research, assisted suicide, living wills, etc. Numerous links to articles, providing worldwide coverage.

http://news.bbc.co.uk/
News and documents from the BBC. Special dossier on euthanasia.

http://www.igsl-hospiz.de
Internationale Gesellschaft für Sterbebegleitung und Lebensbeistand eV (IGSL). International association for end-of-life support and palliative assistance (site in German only).

http://www.dgpalliativmedizin.de/
German Association for Palliative Medicine (some items available in English).

http ://www.drze.de/themen/blickpunkt/sterbehilfe
(English translation available) Page on euthanasia from the science section of the DRZE (German Reference Centre for Ethics in the Life Sciences) website.

http ://www.minbuza.nl/
Multilingual site of the Netherlands Foreign Office containing a questions and answers section setting out government policy on euthanasia.

http ://www.worldrtd.org
The World Federation of Right to Die Societies, housing thirty-seven organisations from twenty-three countries. A great deal of information and many links to other sites.

Appendix III

Recommendation 1418 (1999) of the Parliamentary Assembly of the Council of Europe[1]

Protection of the human rights and dignity of the terminally ill and the dying

(Extract from the Official Gazette of the Council of Europe, 1999)

1. The vocation of the Council of Europe is to protect the dignity of all human beings and the rights which stem therefrom.

2. Medical progress, which now makes it possible to cure many previously incurable or fatal diseases, the improvement of medical techniques and the development of resuscitation techniques, which make it possible to prolong a person's survival, to defer the moment of death. As a result the quality of life of the dying is often neglected, and their loneliness and suffering ignored, as is that of their families and care-givers.

3. In 1976, in its Resolution 613, the Assembly declared that it was "convinced that what dying patients most want is to die in peace and dignity, if possible with the comfort and support of their family and friends", and added in its Recommendation 779 (1976) that "the prolongation of life should not in itself constitute the exclusive aim of medical practice, which must be concerned equally with the relief of suffering".

4. Since then, the Convention for the Protection of Human Rights and Dignity of the Human Being with regard to the Application of Biology and Medicine has formed important principles and paved the way without explicitly referring to the specific requirements of the terminally ill or dying.

5. The obligation to respect and to protect the dignity of a terminally ill or dying person derives from the inviolability of human dignity in all stages of life. This respect and protection find their expression in the provision of an appropriate environment, enabling a human being to die in dignity.

1.
Assembly debate on 25 June 1999 (24th Sitting) (see Doc. 8421, report of the Social, Health and Family Affairs Committee, rapporteur: Mrs Gatterer; and Doc. 8454, opinion of the Committee on Legal Affairs and Human Rights, rapporteur: Mr McNamara).
Text adopted by the Assembly on 25 June 1999 (24th Sitting).

6. This task has to be carried out especially for the benefit of the most vulnerable members of society, a fact demonstrated by the many experiences of suffering in the past and the present. Just as a human being begins his or her life in weakness and dependency, he or she needs protection and support when dying.

7. Fundamental rights deriving from the dignity of the terminally ill or dying person are threatened today by a variety of factors:

i. insufficient access to palliative care and good pain management;

ii. often lacking treatment of physical suffering and a failure to take into account psychological, social and spiritual needs;

iii. artificial prolongation of the dying process by either using disproportionate medical measures or by continuing treatment without a patient's consent;

iv. the lack of continuing education and psychological support for health care professionals working in palliative medicine;

v. insufficient care and support for relatives and friends of terminally ill or dying patients, which otherwise could alleviate human suffering in its various dimensions;

vi. patients' fear of losing their autonomy and becoming a burden to, and totally dependent upon, their relatives or institutions;

vii. the lack or inadequacy of a social as well as institutional environment in which someone may take leave of his or her relatives and friends peacefully;

viii. insufficient allocation of funds and resources for the care and support of the terminally ill or dying;

ix. the social discrimination inherent in weakness, dying and death.

8. The Assembly calls upon member states to provide in domestic law the necessary legal and social protection against

these specific dangers and fears which a terminally ill or dying person may be faced with in domestic law, and in particular against:

i.   dying exposed to unbearable symptoms (for example, pain, suffocation, etc.);

ii.   prolongation of the dying process of a terminally ill or dying person against his or her will;

iii. dying alone and neglected;

iv.   dying under the fear of being a social burden;

v.   limitation of life-sustaining treatment due to economic reasons;

vi.   insufficient provision of funds and resources for adequate supportive care of the terminally ill or dying.

9.   The Assembly therefore recommends that the Committee of Ministers encourage the member states of the Council of Europe to respect and protect the dignity of terminally ill or dying persons in all respects:

a. by recognising and protecting a terminally ill or dying person's right to comprehensive palliative care, while taking the necessary measures:

i.   to ensure that palliative care is recognised as a legal entitlement of the individual in all member states;

ii.   to provide equitable access to appropriate palliative care for all terminally ill or dying persons;

iii. to ensure that relatives and friends are encouraged to accompany the terminally ill or dying and are professionally supported in their endeavours. If family and/or private networks prove to be either insufficient or overstretched, alternative or supplementary forms of professional medical care are to be provided;

iv.   to provide for ambulant hospice teams and networks, to ensure that palliative care is available at home, wherever ambulant care for the terminally ill or dying may be feasible;

v.   to ensure co-operation between all those involved in the care of a terminally ill or dying person;

vi. to ensure the development and implementation of quality standards for the care of the terminally ill or dying;

vii. to ensure that, unless the patient chooses otherwise, a terminally ill or dying person will receive adequate pain relief and palliative care, even if this treatment as a side-effect may contribute to the shortening of the individual's life;

viii. to ensure that health professionals are trained and guided to provide medical, nursing and psychological care for any terminally ill or dying person in co-ordinated teamwork, according to the highest standards possible;

ix. to set up and further develop centres of research, teaching and training in the fields of palliative medicine and care as well as in interdisciplinary thanatology;

x.   to ensure that specialised palliative care units as well as hospices are established at least in larger hospitals, from which palliative medicine and care can evolve as an integral part of any medical treatment;

xi. to ensure that palliative medicine and care are firmly established in public awareness as an important goal of medicine;

b. by protecting the terminally ill or dying person's right to self-determination, while taking the necessary measures:

i.   to give effect to a terminally ill or dying person's right to truthful and comprehensive, yet compassionately delivered information on his or her health condition while respecting an individual's wish not to be informed;

ii. to enable any terminally ill or dying person to consult doctors other than his or her usual doctor;

iii. to ensure that no terminally ill or dying person is treated against his or her will while ensuring that he or she is neither influenced nor pressured by another person. Furthermore, safeguards are to be envisaged to ensure that their wishes are not formed under economic pressure;

iv. to ensure that a currently incapacitated terminally ill or
dying person's advance directive or living will refusing
specific medical treatments is observed. Furthermore, to
ensure that criteria of validity as to the scope of instructions given in advance, as well as the nomination of proxies and the extent of their authority are defined; and to
ensure that surrogate decisions by proxies based on
advance personal statements of will or assumptions of will
are only to be taken if the will of the person concerned has
not been expressed directly in the situation or if there is
no recognisable will. In this context, there must always be
a clear connection to statements that were made by the
person in question close in time to the decision-making
situation, more precisely at the time when he or she is
dying, and in an appropriate situation without exertion of
pressure or mental disability. To ensure that surrogate
decisions that rely on general value judgments present in
society should not be admissible and that, in case of
doubt, the decision must always be for life and the prolongation of life;

v. to ensure that – notwithstanding the physician's ultimate
therapeutic responsibility – the expressed wishes of a terminally ill or dying person with regard to particular forms
of treatment are taken into account, provided they do not
violate human dignity;

vi. to ensure that in situations where an advance directive or
living will does not exist, the patient's right to life is not
infringed upon. A catalogue of treatments which under no
condition may be withheld or withdrawn is to be defined;

c. by upholding the prohibition against intentionally taking
the life of terminally ill or dying persons, while:

i. recognising that the right to life, especially with regard to
a terminally ill or dying person, is guaranteed by the member states, in accordance with Article 2 of the European
Convention on Human Rights which states that "no one
shall be deprived of his life intentionally";

ii. recognising that a terminally ill or dying person's wish to die never constitutes any legal claim to die at the hand of another person;

iii. recognising that a terminally ill or dying person's wish to die cannot of itself constitute a legal justification to carry out actions intended to bring about death.

Appendix IV

Reply from the Council of Europe Committee of Ministers to Recommendation 1418 (1999)

(adopted on 30 October 2000, at the 728th meeting of the Ministers' Deputies)

1. The Committee of Ministers has carefully considered Parliamentary Assembly Recommendation 1418 (1999) on the protection of the human rights and dignity of the terminally ill and the dying and fully shares the Assembly's concerns in this respect. The recommendation raises highly complex problems, which the Committee of Ministers has already considered in various connections, including the 1981 European Health Committee (CDSP) report on care of the dying, the 1988 euthanasia discussions of the Ad hoc Committee of Experts on Bioethics (CAHBI), and the work leading to the adoption of the Convention on Human Rights and Biomedicine (the Bioethics Convention).

2. The Committee of Ministers notes that the Assembly asks it to "encourage the member states to respect and protect the dignity of terminally ill or dying persons in all respects", particularly stressing, first, access to care, including palliative care; second, the terminally ill or dying person's right to self-determination; and, third, the prohibition on intentionally taking the life of a terminally ill or dying person.

3. The Committee of Ministers observes that the CDSP has selected the question of palliative care for a detailed study in 2001. The CDSP intends tackling the question in the wider context of the environment in which palliative care is delivered. The study will look at questions such as over-zealous medical prolongation of life, equal access to health care for old people, professional training in palliative care and reform of medical practice in hospitals and institutions.

4. As regards terminally ill or dying people's right to self-determination, the Committee of Ministers draws attention to Article 9 of the Bioethics Convention, which reads: "The previously expressed wishes relating to a medical intervention by a

patient who is not, at the time of the intervention, in a state to express his or her wishes shall be taken into account." It should be pointed out that this wording reflects the maximum convergence of views among states which took part in drawing up the convention as regards reconciling patient self-determination and medical responsibility.

5.   With regard to the absolute prohibition on intentionally taking the life of a terminally ill or dying person, the Committee of Ministers notes that the legal position differs from one member state to another on advance refusal of certain treatments and on euthanasia. Therefore, with a view to obtaining an overview of laws and/or practices of member states with regard to the issues raised by the recommendation, the Committee of Ministers instructed the Steering Committee on Bioethics (CDBI) to gather relevant information.

6.   Furthermore, the Committee of Ministers stresses that protection of the individual's fundamental rights – including those of the ill or dying – is a matter for the member states, under the supervision, where appropriate, of the European Court of Human Rights. Consequently, the Committee of Ministers has also instructed the Steering Committee for Human Rights (CDDH) to formulate an opinion on Recommendation 1418 (1999).

Appendix V

Reply from the Council of Europe Committee of Ministers to Recommendation 1418 (1999)

(adopted on 26 March 2002, at the 790th meeting of the Ministers' Deputies)

1. The Committee of Ministers welcomes the work carried out by the Parliamentary Assembly, leading to Recommendation 1418 (1999), which addresses the particularly sensitive issues of the protection of human rights and the dignity of the terminally ill and the dying. It recalls its interim reply, adopted on 30 October 2000, informing the Assembly of the terms of reference given to the Steering Committee for Human Rights (CDDH) and the Steering Committee on Bioethics (CDBI).

2. Having closely studied the resulting information and opinion, the Committee observes that member states have varying approaches to the issues dealt with in the recommendation. There are many aspects to these issues – particularly ethical, psychological and sociological aspects – but the Committee of Ministers, committed to the respect and protection of fundamental human rights, intends to restrict itself to the one incontestable area of Council of Europe competence : human rights protection under the European Convention on Human Rights and the case-law of the European Court of Human Rights.

3. Certain issues raised by the recommendation go to the heart of the Convention, particularly regarding Articles 2 (Right to life), 3 (Prohibition of torture and inhuman or degrading treatment or punishment), and 8 (Right to respect for private and family life). Since, as yet, there is no case-law of the Court which could provide precise answers to all the questions raised in the recommendation, the Committee prefers to limit itself to the following points.

4. First, under Article 1 of the Convention, the High Contracting Parties undertake to secure to everyone within their jurisdiction the rights and freedoms defined in the Convention. This is a binding obligation for all Parties, irrespective of any expression of will by the person concerned in this respect.

Therefore, in the case of patients who are entirely incapable of self-determination, the Court has pointed out that they nevertheless remain under the protection of the Convention.[1]

5.   This must be borne in mind when considering the "right of the terminally ill or the dying to self-determination", referred to notably in paragraph 9.*b* of the recommendation. The Committee of Ministers therefore welcomes in this respect paragraph 9.*c* of the Assembly recommendation, to "encourage the member states of the Council of Europe to respect and protect the dignity of terminally ill or dying persons in all respects... by upholding the prohibition against intentionally taking the life of terminally ill or dying persons, while :

i.   recognising that the right to life, especially with regard to a terminally ill or dying person, is guaranteed by the member states, in accordance with Article 2 of the European Convention on Human Rights, which states that "no one shall be deprived of his life intentionally";

ii.   recognising that a terminally ill or dying person's wish to die never constitutes any legal claim to die at the hand of another person ;

iii. recognising that a terminally ill or dying person's wish to die cannot of itself constitute a legal justification to carry out actions intended to bring about death."

6.   There can be no derogations from the right to life other than those mentioned under Article 2 of the Convention. Apart from these cases, no one may be intentionally deprived of life,[2] as the Assembly notes in paragraph 9.*c*.i. The Court has not, however, yet had occasion to rule on the relevance of Article 2 to the proposals set out in paragraph 9.*c*.ii and iii.

7.   As regards the protection of human dignity afforded by Article 3 ("no one shall be subjected to torture or to inhuman or degrading treatment or punishment"), its requirements permit of no derogation.[3] It is true that the Court stated that "as a general rule, a measure which is a therapeutic necessity cannot be regarded as inhuman or degrading",[4] but it also noted that the assessment of an act as ill-treatment falling within the scope of Article 3 "depends on all the circumstances

of the case, such as the duration of the treatment, its physical or mental effects and, in some cases, the sex, age and state of health of the victim, etc."[5] Moreover, Article 3 includes a number of obligations for the state: "Children and other vulnerable individuals, in particular, are entitled to state protection, in the form of effective deterrence, against such serious breaches of personal integrity."[6]

8.   The right to respect for private and family life, as guaranteed by Article 8, would become relevant in some instances, but there are only very rare examples of case-law from the Strasbourg organs that could be linked to questions relating to the dignity of the sick within the scope of such a provision.[7]

9.   The dual objective of alleviating suffering whilst avoiding such violations may give rise to a wide range of national measures. The recommendation draws attention to those concerning palliative care (see notably paragraph *9.a)*. Although definitions of palliative care do exist,[8] the recommendation does not define these terms any more than it gives a definition of the concept of "pain management" mentioned in paragraph 7.i – rightly in the Committee's view, as it does not seem possible to give a uniform European definition of such very broad concepts. The Committee refers in this context to the work being carried out on palliative care by the European Health Committee.[9]

10.   It follows, in the Committee of Ministers' view, that several of the proposals made by the Parliamentary Assembly to member states, in particular a greater commitment on their part to relieving human suffering, can help protect human rights and the dignity of the terminally ill and the dying, provided that the articles of the European Convention on Human Rights mentioned in this reply are respected.

11.   However, in the absence of precise case-law, the question of "human rights of the terminally ill and the dying", seen from the angle of the Convention, gives rise to a series of other very complex questions of interpretation, such as:

–   the question of interplay and possible conflict between the different relevant rights and freedoms and that of the margin of appreciation of the States Parties in finding solutions aiming to reconcile these rights and freedoms;

- the question of the nature and the scope of positive obligations incumbent upon States Parties and which are linked to the effective protection of rights and freedoms provided by the Convention;
- the question of whether the relevant provisions of the Convention must be interpreted as also guaranteeing "negative rights", as the Court has ruled for certain articles of the Convention,[10] as well as the question of whether an individual can renounce the exercise of certain rights and freedoms in this context (and, if that is the case, to what extent and under which conditions).

12. With regard to legislation and practices in member states concerning the problems addressed in the recommendation, the Steering Committee on Bioethics is working on a report, in accordance with the terms of reference assigned to it by the Committee of Ministers. This report, due to be finalised in the course of 2002, will be forwarded to the Assembly in due course. The CDDH, for its part, will follow the development of these issues attentively.

13. In addition, concerning issues related to palliative care, to which the Assembly devoted an important section of its recommendation, the European Health Committee (CDSP) has prepared a study of the situation in many European countries, taking particular account of the contribution made by the Eastern and Central European Task Force on Palliative Care. The CDSP has undertaken to prepare a draft recommendation on these issues. The Committee of Ministers will be apprised of the results of this work in late 2002.

14. The Committee of Ministers wishes at this stage to inform the Assembly that the proposals contained in its Recommendation 1418 (1999) have broadly contributed to the deliberations carried out in this field. Furthermore, the Committee of Ministers welcomes the contacts established between the chairpersons of the competent sub-committee of the Assembly and the Committee of Experts on the Organisation of Palliative Care.

1. European Court of Human Rights, Herczegfalvy v. Austria, 24 September 1992, Series A No. 244, paragraph 82.

2. "(Article 2) not only safeguards the right to life but sets out the circumstances when the deprivation of life may be justified ; Article 2 ranks as one of the most fundamental provisions in the Convention - indeed one which, in peacetime, admits of no derogation under Article 15. Together with Article 3 of the Convention, it also enshrines one of the basic values of the democratic societies making up the Council of Europe. As such, its provisions must be strictly construed", European Court of Human Rights, McCann and Others v. the United Kingdom, 27 September 1995, paragraph 147.

3. Herczegfalvy v. Austria, paragraph 82.

4. Ibid., the Court pointed out that it had to satisfy itself that this necessity had been convincingly shown to exist.

5. European Court of Human Rights, Ireland v. the United Kingdom, 18 January 1978.

6. European Court of Human Rights, A. v. the United Kingdom, 23 September 1998, paragraph 22. States must consequently take legislative or other measures to ensure that individuals within their jurisdiction, especially the most vulnerable - which includes the terminally ill and the dying - are not subjected to inhuman or degrading treatments. Moreover, in a case involving very exceptional circumstances, the Court pointed out that the expulsion of a patient in the terminal phase of Aids to a country where health conditions were unfavourable would constitute inhuman treatment, given that his expulsion would expose him to a real risk of dying in particularly painful circumstances ; see European Court of Human Rights, D. v. the United Kingdom, 2 May 1997, *Reports* 1997-III, No. 37, paragraphs 53-54.

7. European Court of Human Rights, Herczegfalvy v. Austria, paragraph 86 ; European Commission of Human Rights, X. v. Austria, No. 8278, *Decisions and reports* 18, paragraphs 154 and 156 (1979) (blood test), Peters v. Netherlands, No. 21132/93, 77-A *Decisions and reports* 75 (1994) (urine test).

8. The World Health Organisation defines palliative care as "the active total care of patients whose disease is not responsive to curative treatment. Control of pain, of other symptoms and of psychological, social and spiritual problems is paramount. The goal of the palliative care is achievement of the best possible quality of life for patients and their families" (quoted in the Parliamentary Assembly

of the Council of Europe, report on the protection of the human rights and dignity of the terminally ill and the dying, Doc. 8421, 21 May 1999, by Ms Edeltraud Gatterer).

9. This work is mentioned in the interim reply adopted by the Ministers' Deputies on 30 October 2000.

10. For example, for Articles 9 and 11 of the Convention (respectively, the freedom not to have a religion and freedom not to associate with others). (See, for example, the European Court of Human Rights, Buscarini and Others v. San Marino, 18 February 1999, paragraph 34, and European Court of Human Rights Sigurdur Sigurjonsson v. Iceland, 30 June 1993, paragraph 35).

Sales agents for publications of the Council of Europe
Agents de vente des publications du Conseil de l'Europe

TRALIA/AUSTRALIE
ter Publications, 58A, Gipps Street
-3066 COLLINGWOOD, Victoria
(61) 3 9417 5361
(61) 3 9419 7154
ail : Sales@hunter-pubs.com.au
://www.hunter-pubs.com.au

GIUM/BELGIQUE
ibrairie européenne SA
avenue A. Jonnart
?00 BRUXELLES 20
(32) 2 734 0281
(32) 2 735 0860
ail : info@libeurop.be
://www.libeurop.be

de Lannoy
avenue du Roi
I 90 BRUXELLES
(32) 2 538 4308
(32) 2 538 0841
ail : jean.de.lannoy@euronet.be
://www.jean-de-lannoy.be

JADA
ouf Publishing Company Limited
9 Chemin Canotek Road
J-OTTAWA, Ontario, K1J 9J3
(1) 613 745 2665
: (1) 613 745 7660
ail : order.dept@renoufbooks.com
://www.renoufbooks.com

CH REPUBLIC/
UBLIQUE TCHÈQUE
eco Cz Dovoz Tisku Praha
komoravska 21
18021 PRAHA 9
(420) 2 660 35 364
: (420) 2 683 30 42
ail : import@suweco.cz

MARK/DANEMARK
) Direct
staede 31-33
1171 COPENHAGEN K
(45) 33 13 72 33
: (45) 33 12 54 94
ail : info@gaddirect.dk

LAND/FINLANDE
teeminen Kirjakauppa
kuskatu 1, PO Box 218
-00381 HELSINKI
: (358) 9 121 41
: (358) 9 121 4450
ail : akatilaus@stockmann.fi
)://www.akatilaus.akateeminen.com

FRANCE
La Documentation française
(Diffusion/Vente France entière)
124, rue H. Barbusse
F-93308 AUBERVILLIERS Cedex
Tel.: (33) 01 40 15 70 00
Fax : (33) 01 40 15 68 00
E-mail : commandes.vel@ladocfrancaise.gouv.fr
http ://www.ladocfrancaise.gouv.fr

Librairie Kléber (Vente Strasbourg)
Palais de l'Europe
F-67075 STRASBOURG Cedex
Fax : (33) 03 88 52 91 21
E-mail : librairie.kleber@coe.int

GERMANY/ALLEMAGNE
AUSTRIA/AUTRICHE
UNO Verlag
Am Hofgarten 10
D-53113 BONN
Tel.: (49) 2 28 94 90 20
Fax : (49) 2 28 94 90 222
E-mail : bestellung@uno-verlag.de
http ://www.uno-verlag.de

GREECE/GRÈCE
Librairie Kauffmann
28, rue Stadiou
GR-ATHINAI 10564
Tel.: (30) 1 32 22 160
Fax : (30) 1 32 30 320
E-mail : ord@otenet.gr

HUNGARY/HONGRIE
Euro Info Service
Hungexpo Europa Kozpont ter 1
H-1101 BUDAPEST
Tel.: (361) 264 8270
Fax : (361) 264 8271
E-mail : euroinfo@euroinfo.hu
http ://www.euroinfo.hu

ITALY/ITALIE
Libreria Commissionaria Sansoni
Via Duca di Calabria 1/1, CP 552
I-50125 FIRENZE
Tel.: (39) 556 4831
Fax : (39) 556 41257
E-mail : licosa@licosa.com
http ://www.licosa.com

NETHERLANDS/PAYS-BAS
De Lindeboom Internationale Publikaties
PO Box 202, MA de Ruyterstraat 20 A
NL-7480 AE HAAKSBERGEN
Tel.: (31) 53 574 0004
Fax : (31) 53 572 9296
E-mail : lindeboo@worldonline.nl
http ://home-1-worldonline.nl/~lindeboo/

NORWAY/NORVÈGE
Akademika, A/S Universitetsbokhandel
PO Box 84, Blindern
N-0314 OSLO
Tel.: (47) 22 85 30 30
Fax : (47) 23 12 24 20

POLAND/POLOGNE
Głowna Księgarnia Naukowa
im. B. Prusa
Krakowskie Przedmiescie 7
PL-00-068 WARSZAWA
Tel.: (48) 29 22 66
Fax : (48) 22 26 64 49
E-mail : inter@internews.com.pl
http ://www.internews.com.pl

PORTUGAL
Livraria Portugal
Rua do Carmo, 70
P-1200 LISBOA
Tel.: (351) 13 47 49 82
Fax : (351) 13 47 02 64
E-mail : liv.portugal@mail.telepac.pt

SPAIN/ESPAGNE
Mundi-Prensa Libros SA
Castelló 37
E-28001 MADRID
Tel.: (34) 914 36 37 00
Fax : (34) 915 75 39 98
E-mail : libreria@mundiprensa.es
http ://www.mundiprensa.com

SWITZERLAND/SUISSE
BERSY
Route de Monteiller
CH-1965 SAVIESE
Tel.: (41) 27 395 53 33
Fax : (41) 27 395 53 34
E-mail : bersy@bluewin.ch

Adeco – Van Diermen
Chemin du Lacuez 41
CH-1807 BLONAY
Tel.: (41) 21 943 26 73
Fax : (41) 21 943 36 05
E-mail : info@adeco.org

UNITED KINGDOM/ROYAUME-UNI
TSO (formerly HMSO)
51 Nine Elms Lane
GB-LONDON SW8 5DR
Tel.: (44) 207 873 8372
Fax : (44) 207 873 8200
E-mail : customer.services@theso.co.uk
http ://www.the-stationery-office.co.uk
http ://www.itsofficial.net

UNITED STATES and CANADA/
ÉTATS-UNIS et CANADA
Manhattan Publishing Company
468 Albany Post Road, PO Box 850
CROTON-ON-HUDSON,
NY 10520, USA
Tel.: (1) 914 271 5194
Fax : (1) 914 271 5856
E-mail : Info@manhattanpublishing.com
http ://www.manhattanpublishing.com

Council of Europe Publishing/Editions du Conseil de l'Europe
F-67075 Strasbourg Cedex
Tel.: (33) 03 88 41 25 81 – Fax : (33) 03 88 41 39 10 – E-mail : publishing@coe.int – Website : http ://book.coe.int